CONTENTS

Foreword by Second Sea Lord   vii

Foreword by Peter Rogers   ix

Introduction   1

How to use this Book   5

1. **The Six Core Values**   9
2. **The Leadership Context**   25
3. **Leadership Tools**   29
4. **The Operational Context**   33
5. **Twelve Leadership Qualities**   53
6. **Command, Leadership and Management**   63
7. **Leadership in the Future**   87
8. **Insights**   95

Glossary of Terms   135

Acknowledgements   137

Index   141

ROYAL NAVY
WAY OF LEADERSHIP

ANDREW ST GEORGE

ROYAL NAVY
WAY OF LEADERSHIP

preface

Published by Preface 2012

10 9 8 7 6 5 4 3 2 1

First published in Great Britain in 2012 by Preface Publishing

20 Vauxhall Bridge Road
London, SW1V 2SA

An imprint of The Random House Group Limited

www.randomhouse.co.uk
www.prefacepublishing.co.uk

Addresses for companies within The Random House Group Limited can be found at www.randomhouse.co.uk

The Random House Group Limited Reg. No. 954009

A CIP catalogue record for this book is available from the British Library

ISBN 978 1 84809 345 4

The Random House Group Limited supports The Forest Stewardship Council (FSC®), the leading international forest certification organisation. Our books carrying the FSC label are printed on FSC® certified paper. FSC is the only forest certification scheme endorsed by the leading environmental organisations, including Greenpeace. Our paper procurement policy can be found at www.randomhouse.co.uk/environment

Designed and typeset in Vendetta and Frutiger by Peter Ward
Printed and bound in Great Britain by Clays Ltd, St Ives PLC

FOREWORD

By THE SECOND SEA LORD

The sea – and the land which surrounds it – is the natural home of the Naval Service. We operate on it, under it, above it or use it to manoeuvre, ready to go ashore for a variety of government-directed purposes: from humanitarian aid, exclusive economic zone protection, counter piracy, counter narcotics, to war fighting. We must be able to do this worldwide and largely self-supporting. It is both a challenging and hazardous environment, which from the outset requires both deep professional understanding and the highest qualities of leadership; we aim to be the best and must demand the most from ourselves and our people.

So how do we achieve this? We develop our people through experience and training to excel. In particular we develop essential requirements of leadership and teamwork. We also inculcate our core values and standards into our people. These attributes of courage, commitment, discipline, respect for others, integrity and loyalty define our Service. They represent a key element of the moral contract to our people, and although only recently articulated, naval people over the generations would recognise them. Taken together, leadership, teamwork and our values and standards drive our people to achieve the exceptional.

Similarly, we aim to stimulate intellectual capacity in our people, enabling them to challenge the status quo; be curious and encourage new ways of doing things. This breeds a sense of ownership in the service and builds trust. It ensures that the organisation and the people truly understand the future vision – where the organisation is going in the future – why, and what their part will be in achieving excellence. This has contributed greatly to our success in over 550 years.

I commend this book to you, it is the product of three years of research with the willing participation of hundreds of naval personnel; from the most junior at the start of their career, to the most senior, and crucially, from each fighting arm of our service, many with recent combat experience. The pages of this book not only give a strong flavour of what is expected and what can be achieved, but also a good insight into the demanding environment in which we operate. Leadership is a critical life skill, both in the military and in the commercial world; the insights contained within these pages, combined with the benefits of your own experience, provide a solid framework for personnel development and discussion. For us, excellence in leadership is fundamental to our success: past, present and future.

CHARLES MONTGOMERY
Second Sea Lord

FOREWORD

By PETER ROGERS

As Chief Executive of Babcock, I am honoured and delighted to provide my perspective alongside that of the Second Sea Lord in this dual foreword for *Royal Navy Way of Leadership*. Babcock is integrated with Royal Navy ethos and culture in many areas of maritime support services and training development, and is immensely proud of this association. This book, in espousing the Royal Navy's way of leading, has much to offer the commercial sector by way of easily translatable models and examples.

The successful relationship between a large commercial company and the military is dependent on high standards of command, management and leadership. The leadership qualities intrinsic to the maritime arena elicit high professional standards in both civil and naval personnel. Good leadership enables high-quality output from people and equipment. This is absolutely necessary in meeting the challenges of uncertain maritime threats to the United Kingdom's global interests and to international stability.

The importance of the team and of the core values of the Royal Navy are central to everyday business. This book includes views taken across the Service at all levels: from those at sea and ashore, on and under the surface and in the air; from the Royal Marines in all theatres, collectively operating on a global basis every day of the year. Their experiences, humour, can-do attitude and courage reveal what a large family the Royal Navy is, and why as a well-led team they achieve so much.

I am greatly impressed – but not surprised – by the human qualities this book reveals; and I recognise how demanding the 'soft skills' can be. Much depends on trust, integrity, discipline, loyalty and respect for others. These qualities underpin physical courage, fighting spirit and the moral courage to do what is right. Moreover, these are qualities that generate the highest personal standards and the constant drive to be absolutely professional about getting things done, and done to the best of the organisation's collective abilities. It is easy to understand why the Royal Navy is such a professional service and so widely respected wherever the white ensign is flown. It is also apparent how proud its people are to be a part of it and how much successful teamwork matters to them.

This book is essential reading for leaders in the international company I head. As a major partner of the Royal Navy it is important to be as one in culture and values wherever possible. Building trust is the bedrock of successful teams and this degree of trust can best exist on the basis of shared values and ethos.

I thoroughly recommend this book to anyone interested in how important leadership is and with it the proper and thoughtful management of people. This is as true today as it has always been, even with huge advances in technology and methods of conducting war. In the Royal Navy it is the people who are the most important factor; their leadership skills are essential wherever and whenever the Royal Navy is called on to respond.

PETER ROGERS
Chief Executive, Babcock International Group PLC

INTRODUCTION

Sir Edmund Hillary, the first man to climb Everest, once told me that he ranked Antarctic leaders in the following way: for fast and light, Amundsen; for scientific research, Scott; but, when things go badly wrong, for hope, Shackleton. As an Officer, Ernest Shackleton understood that leadership is done by means of the 'soft skills' and not by giving direct orders. Leadership, wherever done, is done by knowing yourself, others, and the situation you are in.

This emphasis on soft skills — emotional intelligence, psychological insight and respect for others — seemed at first surprising in a hugely capable force ready to fight and win on land, at sea and in the air. So why did these skills seem so important? I thought that the Royal Navy's core values and ethos were at the heart of the answer. I therefore embarked on what was to become the largest and most diverse leadership survey ever undertaken by the Royal Navy.

Here was a chance to see first hand what worked and what did not, and to construct a set of principles that were flexible and timeless rather than to create a theory that could not account for or predict all that I found. Leadership theories abound. A choice not to promote any theories or refer to my wide reading of them was not a choice to avoid thinking or observing.

I spent three years with the Royal Navy; I formally listened to over 200 individuals and groups, and informally to countless others. Where they have contibuted formally I have given their rank at the time I spoke to them. I spent time at shore establishments and training centres: I followed leadership instruction and training at all levels of the Royal Navy, from initial induction on HMS Raleigh to strategic planning at The Defence Academy at Shrivenham. I spent time at sea on all types of vessel: aircraft carrier, destroyer, frigate, landing craft, mine-hunter, onshore raiding craft, submarine, fleet auxiliary ships, in land and carrier-based aircraft. I followed officer training at Dartmouth (Royal Navy) and at Lympstone (Royal Marines) and other training establishments such as HMS Collingwood and RNAS Culdrose. From this extended engagement with the Royal Navy I learned the following five things.

First, the Royal Navy excels in rational, timely decision making. The Second Sea Lord (then Admiral Sir James Burnell-Nugent) asked me to write this book (the last of its kind was fifty years ago). He knew that good leadership brings clarity to uncertain situations. Attached to his Royal Navy ID, he carried with him Nelson's Trafalgar Memorandum (9 October, 1805) which is an account of the meeting between Vice-Admiral Nelson and his commanders setting out the plan for engaging the French and Spanish fleets. Burnell-Nugent identified in Nelson's scheme the essence of what the Royal Navy call Mission Command.

1. What is the ultimate objective (the intent)?
2. What means are available (the resources)?
3. Do the means enable the way (the strategy)?
4. As circumstances alter, is there a better way (the contingency)?
5. How do we influence our people to follow (the inspiration)?

Second, the Royal Navy way of leadership has an ethical or moral content. Leadership here appeals not to status or money or preferment but to grounded principles: Commitment, Courage, Discipline, Respect for Others, Integrity and Loyalty. I came to see these qualities as the better parts of human nature amplified, and to value this community because I saw that it valued not only me, but others as individuals.

Third, in the dangerous places to be found at the high end of flying, in the deep end of underwater operations as well as in the hugely complex surface and amphibious environment, great leadership is always clear. That clarity comes from professional expertise combined with an emotional understanding of exactly what it is a commander is asking his or her subordinates to do. This highly effective combination of clarity, judgement and insight invariably gets things done. And it covers both fast and slow thinking – the instinctive decision based on professional judgement and experience, and the strategic decision based on meticulous planning and science.

Fourth, no one follows a pessimist. Cheerfulness (a quality

abundant in Shackleton) is vital in all walks of life, and again this depends on a range of soft skills – respect, knowing others, emotional intelligence – that project an understanding of the scope and range of human experience and situation.

Finally, I realised that Royal Navy leadership is the most accessible and amenable of military styles; and from my work in the commercial sector I see that the Royal Navy way of leadership translates easily and effectively to industry, commerce, charities and government; in fact, to any organisation or task that involves getting people to do things together.

ANDREW ST GEORGE

HOW TO USE THIS BOOK

This book is for those of you in leadership positions, and particularly for officers and senior ratings taking on leadership roles in the Royal Navy. It is principally about the Royal Navy, and not the Royal Marines, but it includes interviews and insights from across the Naval Service. It is designed to be used not only by Royal Navy personnel, but by those who are interested in the way the Navy leads: you may be thinking of joining the Naval Service, or you may be in business, public service, academia or in other areas of life where leadership thinking can be applied.

For the Naval readership, this is a reference for Maritime Through Career Development (MTCD), a handbook for your leadership, and a guide to your thinking. The book defines leadership in a variety of contexts or environments; it sets out the Royal Navy's Six Core Values; it lists twelve fundamental leadership qualities and behaviours; and it details how leadership training takes place throughout your Royal Navy career. You do not have to follow all the advice it offers. In fact, you do not have to read it cover-to-cover. However, you might benefit if you reflect on what it says about leadership in the Royal Navy (and also in the Royal Marines) and apply that thinking to your own position.

The book covers a wide variety of leadership situations. You need to know not only about leadership in your own branch, but also in others. Trust and teamwork are based on the idea that you appreciate what your colleagues are doing and why. In the Dark Blue side of the Royal Navy it makes sense to understand the way that leadership and ethos (how things are done) work in the Royal Marines and in the joint military environment.

The book shows how leadership is underpinned by simple processes (e.g., the maritime estimate) to aid decision making. It also explores how leadership is thought about and practised, not only on the front line but also in other places. Leadership is of paramount importance in planning and allocating resources, the more so when those resources are stretched or diminishing. It is also important for you to know how leadership works on the tactical, operational and strategic levels because you will then better understand and convey your superior's intent.

The chapters that follow are short and contain several checklists; you should add your thinking to them. There are leadership insights in boxes throughout the book, and a selection of longer insights in the second half. These insights and views are not exhaustive. Neither are they mutually exclusive. They relate to their context and to a range of leadership qualities; all are inter-related and inter-dependent: for instance it is not practical to think of courage or commitment in isolation because the two qualities are so closely allied. So the leadership insights represent wider thinking.

Ultimately leadership is about people, and at every level it can be distilled into a set of behaviours or qualities. These behaviours are invariably the best way to handle relationships and – using the related skills of management and the authority of command – are the best way to get things done.

CHAPTER ONE

THE SIX CORE VALUES

Leadership is the ability to apply refined judgement in uncertain situations and to influence others to follow

In the Royal Navy leadership encompasses the cognitive skills, the personal and moral qualities, and the behaviour and military ethos required by commanders to inspire the commitment of others. Leadership is fundamental among the core maritime skills and is developed throughout a career in the Royal Navy.

Leadership exists at all levels, from simple managerial tasks to complex strategic and political planning: the qualities are the same but expressed differently according to the context. Leaders are both born and made: that is, leadership is a combination of inclination and experience, and the product of teaching and learning. Leadership is not a dark art; it can be learned through personal experience and the experience of others, from thinking about the principles involved, and from asking questions and listening to others.

The Royal Navy places high demands on all its personnel, whether at sea, in the air, or on land. These demands are different from those that many people experience in life outside the military. Notions such as service, duty and command are less marked in broader society; conformity to established structures and principles is considered less important than it was in the past; and there is increasingly a market view of social and employment relations that places a higher value on individual rights with less deference paid to authority. In contrast, the business of fighting is essentially a group activity that needs absolute discipline and the subordination of individual rights to those of the team and to the higher purpose of winning the fight.

Cmdre Simon Williams ADC RN Commandant, BRNC Dartmouth

Naval Leadership is essentially about driving a team in a close-knit, often steel-encased floating platform. This essence of leading within a tightly bound structure is the Naval way, and it brings prominence to a mutual reliance between leader and the led which is developed using the Six Core Values of the Naval Service. Of these core values, three most clearly exemplify this mutual, two-way reliance: *Commitment, Loyalty and Respect for others;* whilst *Courage* and *Integrity* are perhaps more personal values, all of course underscored by the *Discipline* necessary in an Armed Force.

This Naval way also has the Divisional System as its

bulwark, dividing the people within a Ship, Submarine or
Naval Air Squadron into small, manageable groups, each led
by a junior officer or senior rating. This system gives personal
responsibility to a young officer for perhaps twenty ratings,
whose welfare, professional performance and capability are
closely managed. Given the nature of the Navy, often deployed
for long periods, this responsibility requires a deeper, more
holistic leadership than in other domains and it depends on
all the Core Values to make it work successfully, perhaps most
particularly *mutual respect*.

Working efficiently, the Naval way of leadership brings
a highly complex and multi layered warship, submarine or air
squadron into a coherent and slick warfighting machine, with
its people working together to provide the Commanding
Officer with the capacity to fight and win.

Leadership within any group tends to alter to match a number of
variables: what the group is doing and where, and its specific situation
and that of the individuals who are part of it. Leadership style derives
from all messages, verbal and non-verbal: how people gesture, sit,
stand, dress, speak, listen and so forth.

Cdr Jeff Short RN (submarine fleet) Training Commander, BRNC, Dartmouth

I need a leader with purpose, clarity of vision, a firm moral compass and loyalty. The loyalty that works both ways and neither shirks from responsibility to admonish or fails to praise when it is due. The moral fortitude to know what is right and where the boundaries exist between what is and is not acceptable behaviour. The clear vision to identify a headmark and set a course to steer that incorporates and absorbs external influences but remains steadfast and true. The sense of purpose and style that creates a positive, unequivocal and lasting impression that others would wish to replicate and take forward as their own.

Leadership derives not only from a set of qualities intrinsic to any leader, but also from the core values shared with all those in his or her team. Taken together, these form a way of seeing and doing – a set of behaviours – based on shared practical means, intellectual approach, moral principles and emotional expression. So the core values are vital to good leadership because they provide the context in which leaders and followers behave. The core values have a moral, ethical and even spiritual dimension, and relate closely to what people believe about themselves and each other.

Core Values + leadership qualities + operational context
= leadership behaviours

The Royal Navy's Six Core Values are: **Commitment, Courage, Discipline, Respect for Others, Integrity** and **Loyalty** (remembered as C2DRIL). These elements of ethos may at first look abstract and staid, but in operational terms, they are current and enduring.

CPO Paul Greenly-Jones (surface fleet) HMS RALEIGH

'Right. You're in the military now. This is how you conduct yourself. This is an order and how you obey it. This is time-keeping. This is discipline. We need your commitment to us, and we will commit to you.' That is the deal. Some people get it instantly; others can't really grasp that for the first few weeks. The core values we've got now are really good. My job is to give an example of each one of them to the trainee or to the recruit as they come through the door.

Your cadets must be able to trust you and trust that what you're saying to them is correct. Anybody can follow orders to the letter, but to trust that what someone's saying is correct is a different sort of trust. That is professional and moral trust.

The Royal Navy's Six Core Values work alongside the enduring spirit derived from people's loyalty to their ship, unit or team, and are sustained by professional standards and strong leadership that promotes courage in adversity and the determination to fight and win. These core values define what a group does and how it does it.

It is worth looking in more detail at the Six Core Values. Leadership and the core values depend on each other; and the core values are fundamental to all aspects of ethos, more so during periods of operations when high morale is necessary for the fighting efficiency of a squadron, ship or unit. Leadership can help address the personal and operational issues that fear, fatigue, discomfort and uncertainty present.

1. Commitment

Selfless personal commitment is the foundation of naval service and enables us to demonstrate a sense of authority and purpose. We must be prepared to serve whenever and wherever we are required, and to do our very best at all times. This means that we accept that we will be expected to put the needs of the mission, and our team, ahead of our own interests.

Commitment to each other, to the task in hand, to the unit or ship, and to the overall intent of command is vital. It defines not only what an individual does, but also how he or she goes about fulfilling their role. It is important that the leader demonstrate a personal commitment to his or her people, to match that of the individual. Commitment is a moral quality with highly practical results.

2. Courage

Courage creates the strength on which fighting spirit, that essential element which turns a fighting force into a winning force, depends. We must have the physical courage to carry on with our task regardless of danger and discomfort, and the moral courage always to do what we know is right.

Courage is an essential core value and informs all the others. Physical and moral courage are the foundation on which bravery, fighting spirit and success are built. Moral courage is of particular significance: it is the ability and willingness to do what is right even though it may be an unpopular course of action; it allows individuals to learn by admitting their mistakes and by accepting responsibility for their actions.

3. Discipline

The Naval Service must be a disciplined service if it is to be effective. We must therefore obey all lawful orders from our superiors. Self-discipline is fundamental; being able to discipline ourselves will earn us the respect and trust of others, and equip us to cope with the difficult, individual decisions we will have to make during our service.

Discipline ensures an environment in which orders are carried out, even under the worst conditions. The fate of a mission and the lives of those who may be thousands of miles away depend on good discipline and on the knowledge that people have done what they should, when they should. In periods of extreme and imminent danger, good discipline can counter fear; along with loyalty and trust of others, discipline can help hold together a team. Self-discipline is one of the most important virtues in the Royal Navy, and tends to be more evident when the conditions are extreme: it derives from a sense not only of professional commitment but from a readiness to put the needs of others and the mission ahead of self-interest.

4. Respect for Others

Each one of us has the exceptional responsibility of bearing
arms, either collectively as part of a unit or individually, and
when necessary of using controlled force. In addition, we will
sometimes have to live and work under extremely difficult
conditions. In such circumstances, it is particularly important
that we show the greatest respect, tolerance, understanding
and compassion for others, regardless of their personal
background; leadership and teamwork depend on it, and
we have the fundamental right to expect to be treated with
the same degree of respect and dignity by all with whom we
serve.

Respect for Others operates up and down the chain of command,
and between peers in a community. Royal Navy personnel treat one
another with decency and fairness, and acknowledge each individual's
contribution to the main effort. The need for high standards of dignity,
compassion and self-control increases as the operating circumstances
become more demanding. In operational environments, individuals
cannot choose the company they keep; conditions may be cramped
or dangerous; and there may be no respite or comfort for extended
periods.

5. Integrity

Integrity is that quality of an individual's character that encompasses honesty, sincerity, reliability and unselfishness. It is an essential requirement of both leadership and comradeship. Unless we maintain our integrity, others will not trust us and teamwork will suffer. Putting this integrity into practice sometimes requires us to show moral courage, because our decisions may not always be popular. This is not always easy; however, doing the right thing will always earn respect.

Integrity is conveyed and tested with every decision and every action; there is always a choice to do the right thing or not. Of course, in a complex and difficult situation there may be a range of options where the 'least worst' is the right course of action. Integrity exudes from character in all dealings with others and with other organisations. It is indicated by qualities such as dependability, punctuality, truthfulness and openness. It is not only essential for the leader of a group to have high integrity; it is vital for the group itself to value and reinforce integrity in individuals and, more widely, in the group and organisation.

6. Loyalty

The Nation, the Naval Service and those with whom we serve rely on our commitment, dedication and support. We must therefore be loyal to our leaders, those that we lead, our team, and our duty. Pass this test and we will never let others down.

Loyalty encompasses allegiance and commitment. It works in many directions: up and down the chain of command, and to ships, units or branches. Loyalty is earned through commitment, self-sacrifice, professional ability, courage and integrity. Those in positions of authority must openly support the policy or strategy set out by higher authority, even if they may personally (rather than professionally) disagree with it; this is not always easy to achieve, but it is nonetheless essential in order to maintain morale and discipline. Good leaders understand the difficulties that can arise here, and the best find ways of overcoming them by demonstrating their professional and moral standing.

Complementing these Six Core Values, the Royal Navy maintains a strong *ethos*. This is simply the way things are done, the essential characteristics of the Service, both formally, and more powerfully, *informally*. Ethos equates to the way people behave towards each other, how they go about their business, and how they present themselves. In the commercial world, it is known as company or corporate culture. Royal Navy ethos is the result of historical, cultural and social influence. It gives people a sense not only of what it means to belong to the Royal Navy, but of how things are done, in spirit as much as in practice.

Determination (an aspect of commitment and integrity) is the willpower to succeed and the driving force to complete a job or operation. This may take the form of mental or physical stamina or resilience, and the resolve to overcome the difficulties inherent in uncertain and dangerous operations. There is often a requirement to go just one step further, refusing to give up through fatigue or fear. In leadership terms, counting on the determination of those in a unit or in a ship is of key importance.

Cdr Liz Walmsley RN Royal Navy Diversity and Inclusion Policy Officer

Great leadership is at the heart of both operational success, and of high achievement and motivation when the demands are less operationally focused. Leadership styles need to be adaptable to the current environment but should always be

---

inclusive. Inclusive leadership embraces, encourages and taps into the creativity and ideas which come from diverse teams. An inclusive leader really gets to know their team, is adaptable and innovative and will allow individuals to be authentic and feel valued for who they are. Inclusive leaders are constructive and supportive, recognise individual strengths and weaknesses and empower their people, giving them the confidence and motivation to perform their best and go that extra mile.

Humour can make the world of difference and banter is an important part of Navy life. But it is the responsibility of all leaders to be alert to the difference between laughing with someone and laughing at them, and the personal line between banter and bullying. A good leader must be prepared to challenge unacceptable behaviour in others and never walk on by.

Humour (an aspect of loyalty and respect), 'banter' and 'spinning dits' are the glue of Royal Navy life. Humour can bring perspective and help people cope with physical hardship, fear or uncertainty. Banter is a game between individuals that all close communities evolve, often a lighthearted way of making a serious point and a sign of acceptance within a group; mutual respect keeps banter in

check, so there is less danger of an individual feeling persecuted. Spinning dits – telling stories with a point – is one of the ways in which ethos is sustained and instilled into new generations of Royal Navy personnel.

Teamwork (an aspect of commitment and discipline) draws together individual components and is fundamental to success. In the era of 'lean manning' in which most people, whether on operations or in the office, have several responsibilities, teamwork is essential in getting things done, sometimes close at hand, and sometimes at great distances.

PO Ady Morton (surface fleet) HMS ARGYLL

You have to lay down the ground rules. When a new lad comes on board, as a Divisional Senior Rating you have to point out to them that there are certain things where they may feel they'll fall by the wayside. It's important to get them early so that they know they've got to work hard before they can do the relaxing and the playing. That is ethos. There is a lot of self-regulating too; we lay the ground rules but then the other lads will help out with a new man, to see he doesn't make errors. For example, you let them know that no matter what happens the working day starts at eight o'clock. We take the day from there.

The 'Can Do' Attitude (an aspect of courage, commitment and discipline) draws on professional expertise, determination, discipline and teamwork in particular. Royal Navy people are adaptable, creative and practical in the way they apply their intelligence to the problems and difficulties inherent in operations. The energy and speed with which they pursue a goal, adapt to overcome a problem, and appreciate the importance of what they are doing are all part of the 'Can Do' attitude. Sometimes when resources are scarce, this positive attitude may mean that people take on more than they can reasonably achieve, but individual efforts are supported by good teamwork and high professional standards. However, one risk of the 'Can do' attitude is a situation where resources cannot meet the promised outcome.

Royal Navy ethos is therefore the way in which the core values will be delivered; leadership is the individual expression of those core values.

Lt Alan Nekrews RN (surface fleet) XO,
HMS HURWORTH

As XO you may have a group of men who might not particularly like you; or they might think you're a reasonable guy. The question is would they follow you? Not 'Do they like you?' but 'Would they follow you?' And if you can answer that honestly and say, 'Yes, I can confidently say, "This group of men would follow me", I don't need to ask them, I just know,' you're probably not far off the mark. And if they would follow you they respect you and would not want to let you down; they would then feel like they were letting themselves down. It is all about your own integrity.

To function as a community of men and women with shared ends, ways, means and risks, certain values – spoken and unspoken – must be recognised and nourished. It is the job of leaders to do that; to find how and where the core values are expressed, and to amplify them.

This then is the broad professional, social and psychological environment in which all leadership takes place. It is important because it shapes and defines standards of behaviour in a range of areas; this behaviour, by and large, is consistent across all branches of the Royal Navy and at all levels of command; yet it also allows for wide individual expression and personal variety, which are part of the richness of service life.

CHAPTER TWO
THE LEADERSHIP CONTEXT

Leadership style should match both the context and the pace of operations. It is therefore fitting that the various operations themselves produce specific leadership behaviours in order to address specific leadership challenges; moreover, the size of a unit and its role can have a profound effect on how it should be led.

Aside from the constraints imposed by the context, there are other important fixed influences. The first is the fact that Royal Navy personnel have a keen appreciation of what their colleagues are doing. The pattern of specialism and posting in the Royal Navy means that personnel understand and value each other's roles. Respect for professional standing and social tolerance in communities also contribute to the sense that others' work is of value and importance. There are also roles – in first aid, damage repair, the divisional system, for example – that bring individuals into contact with others outside their department; this helps build the sense of a community and mutual respect. This combination of knowledge and respect is an invaluable part of all leadership in the Royal Navy.

The second fact is that, looked at in the round, every part of the

Royal Navy depends on some other part of the service. There is little redundancy. For example, just as every part of a ship or submarine is essential to its safe running and effective fighting, so too is the chef who cooks for the crew of any vessel, from an aircraft carrier to a mine sweeper: the quality of food in any community is vital to its physical and moral well-being. In the area of logistics, the supply chain that stretches from vessels thousands of miles from home port to suppliers deep inland is a complex network involving the many variables of time, money, people, equipment, food, fuel and military supplies; one weak link in that chain can at best inconvenience and at worse jeopardise the lives of others. Both are examples of the interdependability of the people in the Royal Navy. While it is possible to isolate one environment, it is clear that, socially, culturally and practically, one person in the Royal Navy depends on the man or woman next to them and on the man or woman perhaps thousands of miles away.

Lt Cdr Laurence Chadfield RN (surface fleet) OC IFT, BRNC Dartmouth

Over my nineteen years of service I have concluded the following: very few Service men and women get up in the morning wishing to fail, not work hard or apply themselves. Their zeal, self-determination and sense of humour never ceases to be inspiring; this is what makes it a privilege to hold the Queen's Commission and lead, often necessitating only the deftest of touches to allow our people to achieve quite astonishing results.

Third, operations with other services are now increasingly interdependent: shared ethos and consistent leadership are vital, particularly in joint training and operations. Moreover, fast-moving, uncertain, ambiguous situations require leadership that can match their speed and complexity. The three distinct levels within military organisations, the tactical (team) level, the operational (organisation) level and the strategic level are less clearly defined in the modern battle space. (There is a fourth level, the military-strategic level that represents the military strand of the political, economic, social and environmental strategies. However, in broad terms, the military strategic level is part of the strategic level). These levels work equally in peacetime operations (humanitarian aid, shipping protection) with the understanding that local tactical outcomes can have immediate strategic implications.

In the new operational environment, individual leadership decisions will tend to have wide and far-reaching consequences. This is one of the most important leadership challenges: as individuals become more responsible, better prepared and better equipped for their roles, particularly in combat, the effect that those individuals can have at both an operational and strategic level is wider and deeper than ever before. Leadership can do more, better, faster; and equally it can make things rapidly go wrong.

In fact, there is rarely a clear practical line between strategic, operational, and tactical levels. *Strategic and tactical leadership overlap*; new technology has made operational leadership more transparent; and tactical effect reaches right up to the strategic level. As tactical units – ships, submarines, aircraft and Marines groups – become more capable and more influential and at the same time operate alongside Army and Air Force (and international joint forces) and in more complex political environments, it is vital that leadership is attuned to the new requirements placed on all three levels.

CHAPTER THREE

LEADERSHIP TOOLS

Aiding the leader in the Royal Navy are some tried and tested tools
for problem solving, and the **Maritime Tactical Estimate** (MTE)
may be one of the most useful. The '7 Questions' or stages of the
MTE follow three broad phases, Analysis (1–3), Course of Action
development and validation (4–6) and the commander's decision (7):

1.   Situational Analysis and effect on the Commander.
2.   Task Analysis – What and Why.
3.   Decide on the effects required and direction necessary to
     develop the plan.
4.   Decide where best to deliver effect.
5.   Identify what resources are required.
6.   Identify the requisite sequencing of actions.
7.   Establish what control measures are required and give direction.

The decision is then conveyed and implemented by subordinates, who are
given the maximum amount of latitude in how they deliver this higher
intent, with an approach that encourages initiative by clear delegation.
The Royal Navy calls this **Mission Command**. All leaders must have an
innate understanding of it in order to appreciate what is being asked of
them and of those they lead. It has the following elements:

1. A commander ensures that subordinates know and understand his / her intentions, their own missions, and the strategic, operational and tactical contexts.

2. Subordinates are told what effects they are to achieve and why this is necessary.

3. Subordinates are allocated sufficient resources to carry out their missions.

4. A commander uses the minimum of control so as not to limit unnecessarily his / her subordinates' freedom of action.

5. Subordinates decide for themselves how best to achieve their missions.

6. The commander sets boundaries and a system for reporting back on progress.

Alongside these, the leader's communication skills, clarity, vision, and understanding of the capabilities of individuals and the effect or orders are central to the leadership challenge. The Tactical Estimate and Mission Command are together a powerful way of dealing with fast-moving and uncertain situations. Proper use of them is fundamental to any leader's intellectual and practical understanding and judgement. Orders are conveyed using a standard format, understood internationally amongst member states: the **NATO Sequence of Orders**.

PO Tim Cordery (surface fleet) SRCC, RNLA,
HMS COLLINGWOOD

The NATO Sequence of Orders is an effective leadership tool.
Certainly it can be applied to anything. Once somebody
applies NSOs to any given task, be it loosely or to the letter,
then they're on to a winner because they have applied thought.
NSO is a thought process; once you get that process into
your head, it becomes natural. Use NSOs and the underlying
process and it should become second nature; it doesn't matter
what plan, just apply NSOs, and get an answer; nine times out
of ten, the right answer.

This is an important leadership tool in that it makes all aware of the
situation, what needs to be done, and how the end will be achieved. A
good delivery of these orders – in an appropriately assertive and calm
manner – will leave no room for confusion:

1. Preliminaries (seating, map coordinates, terrain, weather);
2. Situation (title of operation, friendly forces, enemy forces);
3. Mission;
4. Execution (brief, preparations, transit to target, actions on
   target, return to base, debrief);
5. Support Issues (food, accommodation, dress etc);
6. Command and Communications;

7. Safety;

8. Questions; and

9. Next Iteration.

These ways and means of conveying intent and detailing orders have one aim: clarity. This is essential to leadership and to the proper exercise of command. In any situation a leader should be able to analyse the situation, plan and weigh up a course of action, and convey his / her intent or instructions using Mission Command in a brief set of orders. This is a leadership skill that should be developed to a very high level and is crucial in the crowded and fast-moving modern battle space.

Lt Cdr Zoe Briant-Evans RN RNLA

For me, leadership is the single most important quality in any officer. Whether in a training environment, or on the bridge of a warship, your people should not only be inspired to follow you, but to achieve the very highest standards themselves. As an officer, you should never forget that you will be expected to take the lead. In my experience the maritime environment is a rapidly changing one. Even if a situation appears benign, it can rapidly develop into a crisis. If this is the case, you can be sure that all eyes will turn to you, and you should always be ready for it.

CHAPTER FOUR

THE OPERATIONAL CONTEXT

LEADERSHIP IN THE FLEET

The ships, submarines and aircraft of the Royal Navy carry out a wide range of tasks. An aircraft carrier, for example, is able to conduct air operations against land targets, air support of ground forces, defensive and offensive operations against enemy air power, support of amphibious units, helicopter operations, communications and command and control of a task force, humanitarian and disaster relief, defence diplomacy and peace support operations. Submarines may be operating against other submarines, or firing cruise missiles against land targets and this sort of multi-role flexibility is also found in frigates, destroyers, assault ships, mine-hunters and hydrographic vessels. The leadership challenges vary in importance and urgency in each case; the potential variety of operations is almost limitless.

A fighting ship or submarine is a *community of people*. It is easy to run an efficient ship (or department or mess within it) that is unhappy, or a happy ship (or department or mess) that is inefficient. The challenge for those in leadership is to strike the balance between the two. Leadership in this regard is a combination of personality and vision; this is distinct from management (more a matter of calculation, statistics, methods, timetables and routine). Managers are necessary, leaders are essential.

The community life of a ship or boat has three important aspects. First, depending on the size and design of the ship, the crew lives alongside each other at close quarters. *Integrity, loyalty and respect are vital here.* This is particularly relevant for Leading Hands and the Leading Hands of the Mess who live with those they are charged with overseeing. Here, there is no hiding place and no stopping place. A Leading Hand may well be in a bunk alongside someone he or she has had to discipline. It is one of the key leadership skills to be able to *separate the people from the issues.*

The second aspect of community life in the fleet is the very high degree of *trust* that must exist between all members of the crew. Men and woman at every level in the ship's management must foster trust *up and down* the chain of command and *between* departments. Trusting others – and by implication the training and professional knowledge they have received – is another key leadership skill which balances risk, delegation and knowledge of the individual (and oneself). Discipline and commitment are of high value here.

LOM Peter Garrow (surface fleet) HMS PROTECTOR

As for being Leading Hand of the Mess: if you ask any Leading Hand, it's probably the hardest job to do. You're in charge of the whole Mess Deck. If you live in Portsmouth during the week the ship's alongside you go home at night but you're still the one who's in charge of the Mess even though you're not there. So anything that happens in that Mess, whether you're there or not, it's your neck on the line. That means you have to delegate and trust; and the Mess has to trust you.

Good leaders are inspirational, good motivators; they lead by example. Good morals are probably less important. I try to be cheerful. If you're not cheerful you're not approachable. And as a leader – there are many different leaders, completely different – it all comes from your character. Everyone is completely different in their leadership style so I try to be approachable, cheery, lead by example; personal qualities come into it as well.

The third aspect of life in the fleet is *morale*. Leaders at all levels need to be positive and cheerful. A ship's company quickly absorbs and reflects (even amplifies) the mood of the Captain and senior officers. The middle managers of the ship – the Chiefs and POs – have a crucial role here in maintaining a positive outlook and conveying as much information as possible to the crew. In times of fear and fatigue every nuance of expression – in words, in body language and in action – will be scrutinised by all those around the ship's leaders. Good leaders develop the sense of when to speak directly to their people and in doing so show the quality of their leadership.

***

WO2 Tony Starbuck (surface fleet) HMS HURWORTH

It is amazing how much information you learn in a scran queue. I stand up by the scran queue, and watch the lads go in: 'How you doing? No problems? Have you got any snags or anything like that?' And you just listen. That is part of leadership for me because I need to know and care about my people.

***

Finally there is a wide range of items which occupy all leaders onboard: the ship's operational capability, the safety of the ship, competence of the crew, state of machinery and weapons, security, training, fire prevention, damage control and risk assessment. Aside from the practical implication in each area, the hundreds of classified books, documents and signals that these entail can be overwhelming. In each area there are absolute standards; however, time, resources, logistical constraints and operational urgency may well mean that a solution is at best temporary or at worst unavailable. Here, the key leadership skill is the *assessment of risk* and the willingness to take responsibility for decisions.

LEADERSHIP IN OPERATIONS

Naval Leadership is essentially about team leadership. Leading within a tightly bound structure is the Naval way. Much of the Navy's planning and execution takes place in the office, in training establishments, and on land bases; this environment should not be overlooked or underestimated, because leadership of close teams continues here.

Effective work everywhere requires precise and thoughtful handling of relationships, communications, responsibilities and authority, resources, teams and, of course, oneself. What is true here works well in all non-combat environments: on bases, on shore establishments and in engineering, procurement, instruction or in peacekeeping, disaster relief, and many more. In times of high activity, planning and execution depend on high levels of efficiency and intelligence; in times of scarcity or rebalancing, leadership away from the front line takes on a special importance and motivation and direction need to be given for teams with decreasing resources and increasing workloads.

There are several key *relationships*. Relations with superiors tend to work better when there is proper delegation, clarity, trust, respect and understanding. Relations with deputies, with section heads and with team members need to be conducted evenhandedly and with clarity. Superiors must be approachable, give due credit and appreciation for good work, and understand the pressures on individuals and on their teams.

Cdr Kieran O'Brien RN (aviation) Commander Air
Engineer, HMS ILLUSTRIOUS

Recognising what I'm here for is vital. I know how the
department should be run. I've been a Junior Officer working
in aviation so I know what all the roles are supposed to do
and I understand where my position is. I can do all their jobs.
The comfort zone is a regression to what you knew before, so
you may be pulled backwards in your thinking: 'I can make
decisions on tactical stuff, day-to-day, because I did that
fifteen years ago, I can do that sort of thing.' You feel young
again, actually, doing that sort of stuff. But I have people who
do that for me. My job is to look ahead.

Communications must be straightforward and simple, supported by
team meetings and internal communications every day. It is vital that
there is a shared sense of who is doing what and when: this avoids either
overlapping or discontinuous work. In all communications, clarity is
the first and last rule; in giving instructions, complex requirements
should be written out. Supervisors should be alert to early signs of
confusion and misunderstanding. In getting ideas across (rather
than instructions), it is vital to work hard to find out whether an
idea is fully understood and, if resisted, why. If a piece of work needs
to be done quickly but not thoroughly or must focus on intellectual

content rather than presentation style, this must be made clear from the start.

Lines of *responsibility*, *authority* and *accountability* should be clear. Each team member will have a written account of his / her responsibilities; it is usually good practice for team members to see each other's responsibilities, especially if some responsibilities extend beyond the standing command arrangements. Authority varies between team members. A good leader makes sure that delegated authority is written down, understood and matched by responsibility. Authority has a wider sense in office life: up and down the hierarchy, no one should expect to be undermined. Over time, a confidence develops, fostered by consistent behaviour and plain dealing. Accountability is simple: it must match responsibility. That is clearly understood by all members of the team.

Cdr Alec Parry RN (surface fleet) Commander Logistics, HMS ILLUSTRIOUS

You don't get anything from screaming and shouting at people. Although there is a time when you have to deliver something with force because of the urgency of getting things done immediately. In day-to-day business I don't bark orders at people because there's just no need. I've got a Lieutenant Commander who's very capable, five Lieutenants who are

---

> all growing all the time in their expertise. And I've got two
> Warrant Officers and six Chiefs – that's an awful lot of horse-
> power, an awful lot of highly paid people, plus all their own
> teams, all working on one thing – which is the ship. I'm fiercely
> loyal and protective of everybody in my department. We're all
> part of one big group and I'm privileged to sit on top of it.

Resources have to be made available for the team and individuals to
carry out their responsibilities. Resources are not only time, money,
staffing and equipment; they are also skills and working conditions.
The demand for resources always outstrips supply; this mismatch can
be addressed by prioritising work and making sure that the working
environment enables each individual to do the best work they can.

Leaders in charge of *teams* must deal honestly in terms of
performance. Honesty over such absolutes as money and security are a
given. Giving advice, criticism and handling the hopes and ambitions
of subordinates requires absolute honesty coupled with high emotional
intelligence. A good leader devotes time and effort to telling members
of his/her team how they are doing and how to do better. Appraisal,
report writing, recommendations for promotion and dismissal require
careful, early thought and exact expression.

Finally, it is vital to be able to handle *one's own emotions* and to
present a range of behaviours which are fair, decent, reliable, polite

and, above all, consistent. Team members have to be able to express and convey their leader's views and carry out his/her wishes with the confidence that they will receive support should the need arise. Conversely, an inconsistent leader has a debilitating effect on a team. Decisiveness, reliability, trust and good manners are all important to the consistent leader.

Cdr Andy Hancock RN (BRNC) The Commander, BRNC Dartmouth

The ability to inspire is an essential element of good leadership. I believe that the three components of military power can be mapped across to the three components of inspirational leadership. The intellectual component is the ability to have a clear, realistic vision that is easily communicated to the followers; the moral component is emotional – the passion required to enthuse followers to believe in the leader's vision; and finally the physical component being the energy to drive that vision to a conclusion, which includes a physical presence and determined example being set by the leader.

Great leaders delegate. This is particularly so in an office, where there is a temptation to intervene and micro-manage. Delegation is balanced by involvement and varies according to projects; the key decision is taken at an early stage: to be involved or not. The later arrival of an interfering leader in a complex project is unhelpful. Delegation is enabled by a mix of staff capability and training, professional competence, emotional intelligence and individual confidence.

Naval Leadership is about running and influencing small teams *at every level*: this might be an engineering team tasked to solve a problem, a damage control team faced with fire or flood, a medical team dealing with casualties, or a strategic planning team operating and coordinating ships, submarines and aircraft or a strategic planning team. The leadership qualities do not change, nor do the core values. However, environment affects people, and because leadership is all about people, leaders must take account of it.

Each context produces subtly different forms of professional exchanges within and between teams, shaped by the urgency, arduousness and danger of each mission in a particular ship, boat or aircraft. The Six Core Values always inform the way that leaders and teams behave, and allow for variations both within any environment (as circumstances change) and across the many environments in which the Navy operates. Therefore, it is worth exploring some of the distinct contexts that in turn produce distinctive ways of getting things done, all consistent with widely accepted Six Core Values.

THE SURFACE FLOTILLA

The Surface Flotilla operates across the widest spectrum of warfare disciplines, including Air Warfare, Surface Warfare and Underwater Warfare, together with Aviation, all conducted simultaneously. In practice this might mean shelling a land target using the medium calibre gun in support of land forces, protecting vulnerable shipping from small boat attack, countering a submarine threat, dealing with enemy aircraft firing missiles and getting the correct wind and posture to launch and recover helicopters whilst managing enough electrical power to supply a small town, balancing four powerful engines, supplying ammunition from deep magazines and cooking food for everyone – simultaneously. Within a single operations room in an individual ship there are teams focusing on each part of this battle, led by senior ratings, and they are brought together and prioritised by a Principal Warfare Officer (PWO). In turn this warfare effort is supported closely by teams of Engineers and Logisticians.

Each of these teams and specialisations exhibit their own 'tribal' characteristics – be they Chefs, Stokers or Gunners – and thus within this team of teams leadership is focused on the shaping of these potentially disparate areas into a cohesive warfighting whole, building on the fact that they are all very literally in the same boat. Despite the range of disciplines in this complex system it is the similarities, rather than the differences, which define a fighting ship's company.

The good Commander will know his people and will communicate the command aim clearly and simply, relying on high standards of training to allow the ship to work like a well-oiled machine.

ROYAL MARINES

Almost a quarter of the Naval Service are Royal Marines, who operate in a wide range of environments. The scope of their experience from diverse operations carries useful lessons for those working alongside them. Several factors have a bearing on the way their leadership supports their operational expertise, and it is helpful for any Naval leader to understand the operational context for a compatriot in the Royal Marines.

Brig Bill Dunham RM (Royal Marines) Commandant, CTCRM Lympstone

Leadership should not be treated as a separate subject.

Leadership should be treated as something intrinsic to the work that you're doing so you can show leadership in all sorts of different ways. You show leadership by the way that you present yourself; by the standards that you set (even when you're not in a direct leadership role); by having a deep

---

knowledge of your profession; by being able to articulate that deep knowledge; by setting a personal example in all sorts of ways. It needs to be internalised, something everybody buys into.

You can teach techniques which will help in your leadership and way of doing things. Many people want to come to us to pick up leadership. Actually what we do with most of them in terms of leadership is give them a structure around which to base their activity, take them outside the comfort zone that they're used to, and simply ask them to complete tasks. There's nothing fancy about it.

It is important to understand the ways in which the Royal Marines describe their *ethos*; this is seen as both individual (courage, determination, unselfishness and cheerfulness in the face of adversity) and collective (unity, adaptability, humility, professional standards, fortitude and commando humour). Ethos is deeply felt and understood throughout the Corps; and it is innate in all operations and training. In leadership terms, shared ethos produces an immediate, unspoken understanding between all Marines; and shared values mean that leaders at every level can rely on a set of qualities and behaviours in the Marines around them; it also allows Marines to communicate leadership and ethos by non-verbal means: military bearing, readiness for action, body language. Royal Marine ethos equates to the Core

Values of the Navy; any question of what to do, how to do it, and when, can be answered by referring to ethos: it is simply the way that things get done.

Capt Chris Burr RM (Royal Marines) Royal Navy Leadership Academy (RNLA), Dartmouth

Over my seven thoroughly rewarding years in the Royal Marines I have had the privilege to command (directly and indirectly) 300 Marines and deploy three times to Afghanistan with them. I have shared both highs and lows with them and I have been continually humbled by their utter professionalism, courage, and fortitude in the most dire of circumstances. Their diligence, unquestionable loyalty, and humble approach has inspired me to produce the best standard of work I possibly can and I have continuously tried to better myself in order to perform as a commander of these men.

Marines tend to work in small groups (the more specialised the operation the smaller the group); this in turn means that high responsibility is placed on young and junior Marines. Leadership here must be clear, determined and forthright; it must also be agile, politically sensitive and tactically aware in modern combat. Royal Marines find themselves on politically sensitive missions that are at the same time both tactically and strategically important. There is the *blurred distinction in the crowded modern battle space* between the team / tactical level, the organisation / operational level and the strategic level. The moral and intellectual elements of leadership are here vital. In conducting operations among the people, in winning hearts and minds and at the same time achieving military objectives and wearing down the will of the enemy, a single mistake could influence an entire campaign.

PO Tim Hall (surface fleet) Coxswain,
HMS HURWORTH

Leadership of small groups is subtle. You put your diver in and have a standby diver there waiting to help; he has to commit himself to whatever is required. The supervisor is at the back of the boat with the weight of the world on his shoulders. The diver has an obligation to himself in the water, to remember his drills and to make sure he doesn't put his supervisor and the standby diver in a compromising position. Trust works both ways and is essential.

Difficult amphibious operations, complex joint-forces operations, extremes of heat or cold, urban and wilderness environments all require different kinds of resilience and stamina in leaders. In these situations, basic living conditions may be extremely tough; mental morale and physical fitness are vital in prevailing and imposing will on the situation. The Royal Marines' success in these environments requires high levels of commitment and courage.

FLEET AIR ARM

Leadership in the Fleet Air Arm is invariably in small groups where the safety of others is paramount. Flying is inherently dangerous. This single overwhelming fact means that leadership has to be calm, rational and understated. For those working in small, highly trained groups in both operating and maintaining the aircraft, levels of trust are at a premium. In terms of safety, any faults or mistakes tend to have sudden and swift consequences and there is little time to rectify them in the air. *The high levels of professional excellence and consequently high levels of integrity and discipline are intrinsic to Fleet Air Arm operations.*

The second influence on leadership is the *wide diversity in the use of air power.* The Fleet Air Arm provides a multi-role combat capability that can operate at short notice in all environments, day and night, over land and sea. Helicopters fulfill a wide variety of roles, from search and rescue to surveillance, communications, anti-submarine and attack. Each sortie requires the closest teamwork not only between the crew of the aircraft and the ship's operations team, but also between teams of ground technicians, weapons engineers, communications and intelligence specialists, and aircraft handlers on ships and on shore.

Lt Alexandra Kelley RN (Observer) RNAS CULDROSE

One of the most important roles as an Aircraft Commander is having the ability to effectively lead and manage your crew in order to accomplish the designated mission. Each crew member is an expert within their own field but without the necessary leadership, ineffective as a single entity in completing the task. The key to achieving a successful sortie is creating a cohesive team that can often range in experience and seniority, who feel comfortable working together within a dynamic, high pressure environment and who have confidence in your decisions.

The third major determinant of leadership style is the *structure of the Air Squadrons*. These relatively small communities live and work closely together; people tend to identify strongly with their Squadron, and, much in the same way as the Royal Marines, a strong and beneficial ethos evolves. An unspoken set of shared values and standards is part of the working and community life of the Squadron.

Finally, *aviators use the Estimate Process in planning each sortie*; this is adapted for particular use in the air environment where variables such as flight time, fuel, weather, weapons etc must be allowed for. The Estimate is constantly reviewed during a sortie; and aviators make extensive use of a debrief on their return to base to highlight – ideally in a completely 'no fault' way – any operational anomalies or safety issues that may have arisen during the flight. The consistent use of rational planning, flexible operation and meticulous debriefing (supported by a 'no-fault' system) all give opportunities for an informal and understated leadership style to exist alongside the more formal procedures.

SUBMARINES

There are two dominant factors that shape the style of leadership on board a submarine. The first is *the priority of safety*, not only of the boat's hull and nuclear reactor but also of its navigational instruments, its means of changing depth and direction, and its weapons. Many of the exchanges on board are delegation and instruction as crew members pass on their full-ship knowledge to new crew who must qualify as a submariner by earning their 'Dolphins'. The badge represents a level of technical knowledge which is the direct result of the overwhelming priority of safety on board. *Mutual respect, commitment and integrity are absolute.*

The *high level of professionalism* in operating and navigating the boat is another aspect of the priority of safety. A submarine must be constantly adjusted and trimmed, unlike a warship; it must move in three dimensions and listen while itself remaining unheard in tracking other submarines, in carrying out surveillance or beach reconnaissance, for example. These activities require unstintingly high levels of professional competence and unwavering concentration. Good leaders can recognise when a crew is working at its limits rather than within them.

Lt Cdr Dave Burrell RN (submarine fleet) Navigation instructor, BRNC Dartmouth

A submarine is a uniquely autonomous unit, with a close-knit crew working in close confines. As such the greater part of my inspiration onboard comes from those you work for an d with. From the peerless example of Command in the face of adversity at one end of the spectrum to the newly joined AB working tirelessly to achieve his 'Dolphins' at the other. When the tempo is high no one wants to be the one that lets down his shipmates and when it is quieter that same Ship's Company rely on you to keep them safe as they sleep in their bunks, which is all the inspiration I have ever needed.

The second leadership factor is *the close community nature of a submarine*. The combination of claustrophobia, the absence of daylight, sleep deprivation, lack of privacy, space and exercise, amounts to a sustained psychological ordeal. Over time, tolerance and respect for others can be tested to the limit. Successful submariners tend to be able to be relaxed and informal. They take account of all the demands on them – professional excellence in face of objective dangers, psychological anxiety, and social issues – and nonetheless manage to remain cheerful, friendly and relaxed. Each boat develops a strong ethos, set by the Captain and Executive Officer.

In any place in the Navy, therefore, leadership is essentially about running and inspiring close-knit teams. Those teams can be at work on or under the sea, on land, or in the air. What all have in common is a mutual reliance between leader and the led which emerges from the Six Core Values of the Naval Service, three of which – Commitment, Loyalty and Respect for Others – are fundamentally reciprocal in nature.

CHAPTER FIVE

TWELVE LEADERSHIP QUALITIES

Leadership is the ability to apply refined judgement in uncertain situations and to influence others to follow

All successful armed forces and many commercial organisations adapt and transform faster than their opponents. The Royal Navy is conducting more complex operations than at any time in its history. Military doctrine over the last generation has evolved quickly to encompass complex combat operations involving joint initiatives, interagency liaison and multinational teams. What constitutes military operations is changing fast: counter-piracy, cyber attack and defence, counter-terrorism, information dominance and 'non-kinetic' effects.

In the twenty-first century, conflicts have tended to have particular characteristics. Military operations are used increasingly for establishing the conditions for a political outcome (and not for hard objectives). War is conducted amongst the people (i.e., in communities) rather than on the battlefield. Ships, for example, fight from busy shipping lanes with commercial air traffic above and have to overcome all the uncertainty and ambiguity this brings. The military fights to preserve rather than risk its own people and resources. The sides in modern conflicts can be shifting and often comprise non-state and international participants; and finally conflicts tend to be timeless or apparently unending and insoluble.

Admiral Sir Mark Stanhope (submarine fleet)
First Sea Lord and Chief of the Naval Staff

The measure of leadership is the judgement call. One of the good things about the military is that easy judgement calls are made lower down. When the difficult judgement calls come up, by definition they are more complex, more ambiguous. 'How am I going to make a decision on this?' There is no right answer. So you're making a judgement call on lots of other factors. Judgement is about intellectual skills, which you can teach. However, judgement in a military context is as much about experience as it is about intellectual prowess.

This set of complex conditions requires an agile and flexible approach; thinking may change in terms of tactics and strategy, sometimes rapidly and radically. What follows from this situation is a need for principles that underpin thinking at every level and in every encounter in peace and in conflict. Ethos and leadership together provide a number of principles for action.

Leadership can be taught, learned and improved through practice by anyone prepared to make the effort. In that regard, it is no different from any other professional skill required in the Royal Navy. It is beyond doubt a skill – or more properly, a set of skills – learned more easily than taught. The reason is that each individual alone knows best his or her own work conditions and capabilities: everyone does it differently. This is why this book contains leadership insights from men and women from a variety of branches and ranks in the Royal Navy.

The operational context at sea, in the air, and on land, produces different emphasis on leadership behaviours. There are twelve core leadership qualities that every leader must have, although not all are needed in every situation.

These twelve qualities are leadership behaviours that work. They do not come naturally to everyone, but all great leaders have these in some measure, or understand that they need to be demonstrated at the appropriate time. These qualities form a complex inter-relation; some are intrinsic to character, others drawn out by the needs of the situation. They are deliberately not weighted here as their importance and relevance will change with the situation, and are simply listed alphabetically:

1. Capacity for Judgement and Decision Making

The ability to judge, decide and convey that decision succinctly and persuasively depends on high levels of thoughtfulness and intellect, and on the ability to decide and to act fast. Timely decisions are vital in all contexts, but never more so than when a situation is uncertain or changing rapidly, so both clarity and speed are key elements in a rounded capacity for making and conveying decisions. Planning effectively, assessing risks and then making judgements in a timely manner – the speed must match the context – is a combination of professional knowledge, confidence and clear thinking.

2. Cheerfulness

No one follows a pessimist and a sense of humour is part of Royal Navy ethos. Particularly in circumstances that are adverse, uncertain or frustrating, both general cheerfulness and specific humour can be of immense benefit to morale. A gloomy or a cheerful view of a situation is a conscious choice, even if the circumstances lie beyond the control of individuals: in extreme weather, difficult operational conditions or during periods of uncertainty in programmes, cheerfulness is a vital asset.

3. Clarity and Vision

The key aim of any leader is clarity of intent so that people know where they stand and 'what the boss wants and means'. For this, the leader must be clear about his or her vision of how things will be. The leader must then give clear and unambiguous guidance on areas that are theirs to decide and sort out any logjams of confusion. The technique needs to be tailored to the circumstances; what may be appropriate for the commander of a maritime group where there is daily separation from subordinate commanders may not work in an MOD job. In essence, this principle can be summed up as 'know your people' in order to make yourself clear to them.

4. Communications skills

Great leaders communicate in all ways: by the way they stand, speak, write and work. However, great leaders are also great listeners and observers; these two skills are vital in communications. To be able to see and hear clearly what is going on – practically and emotionally – and to distil and convey that understanding to others is a rare skill. Good communications skills combine practical and emotional intelligence.

5. Confidence

Confidence in others and in oneself is a key element of leadership. Confidence in others derives from trust built up through personal knowledge, professional competence and good working relationships. The Royal Navy has a well-developed system of delegation and training to foster confidence and trust up and down the command chain. In addition to the confidence that men and women in the Royal Navy have between each other, confidence in one's own abilities is essential for good leadership.

6. Humanity and Humility

The other leadership qualities cannot display themselves without this quality. Another term for this is 'emotional intelligence' or the ability to gauge the effect of one's own personality – and those of others – on any situation. It encompasses understanding, good manners and respect for others; also tolerance of difference in manner and opinion. At close quarters, a clear understanding of why one person is bold while another may be hesitant is of great value in leadership.

7. Innovation

Being innovative, creative, resourceful, agile and sometimes
lateral rather than direct are qualities that are of vital
importance in all three management areas: daily operations,
tactical execution and strategic planning. All conflict is by
definition uncertain and fast-paced; people who can embrace
rapidly changing environments, rules of engagement and
different forms of threat and new forms of warfare will be at a
premium. Innovation here is vital, as a truly creative leader can
manage change, bring fresh insights, take risks and encourage
others to do likewise.

8. Integrity

Integrity and trustworthiness are important moral standards.
They are conveyed and tested with every decision and every
action; there is always a choice to do the right thing or not. Of
course, in a complex and difficult situation there may be a range
of options where the 'least worst' is the right course of action.
Integrity exudes from character in all dealings with others and
with other organisations. It is indicated by qualities such as
dependability, punctuality, truthfulness and openness. It is not
only essential for the leader of a group to have high integrity;
it is vital for the group itself to value and reinforce integrity in
individuals and, more widely, in the group and organisation.

9. Moral and Physical Courage

Moral courage is a rare quality, and essential for leadership. Moral courage is the ability to speak clearly and truthfully, sometimes counter to prevailing wisdom or against the momentum of a decision or plan. Moral courage tends to become stronger with use, as people become more confident about themselves and about the real benefits of doing the right thing. Royal Navy ethos here is of great significance, as moral courage tends to be candid and plain in expression: so trust and respect for others are paramount. Many branches foster moral courage by having a 'no fault' or 'no blame' culture, or by cultivating an ethos in which no question is too small or too stupid. Physical courage can be developed in any individual, learned and copied from others; it is based on trust in others, a professional assessment of risk, and the commitment to get things done.

10. Professional Knowledge

All other leadership qualities depend on this foundation. In any situation at sea, in the air, on land, whether executing, planning or persuading, almost everything depends on the quality and credibility of an individual's professional knowledge. Intelligence here is vital. It may well be that he or she does not have an intimate knowledge of the situation, but there will be nonetheless a professional judgement that comes from knowing exactly what is being asked of the team, and what will be the effect on the team of the command decision. Professional knowledge of course encompasses knowledge of people, politics, tactics and strategy as well as a narrower technical knowledge. High professional standards are essential for present efficiency and future success. The Royal Navy trains, coaches and mentors individuals to high levels of professional excellence throughout their careers; promotion and advancement in the Royal Navy depends on passing professional exams or courses and by competitive selection. In those respects the Royal Navy is a professional meritocracy. High levels of delegation and trust encourage individuals to learn, to assume responsibility and to instruct others both formally and informally. Professional standards are therefore central to how the Royal Navy operates.

11. Stamina

Most great leaders have stamina, both physical and moral, which makes them highly resilient as individuals. They tend not to give up, they tend not to worry about minor setbacks, and they tend not to be intimidated by uncertain or fast-moving situations. There is no doubt that physical stamina is highly important in all branches of the Royal Navy; it enables individuals to remain physically and intellectually alert for long periods, to recover quickly from tough operations, and to sustain demanding schedules over long periods. Leaders may be 'first up' and 'last down', particularly when conditions require them to find space for thinking and planning, but in a more protracted operation the good leader will pace himself or herself to retain the necessary reserves.

12. Trust

The ability to trust and be trusted as an individual, a team or a unit, is fundamental to good leadership and to good comradeship. Trust works at many levels: up and down the chain of command, and between peers. High levels of trust are required in dangerous operational environments or in difficult training programmes. Trust can take many forms: emotional, moral, intellectual, professional and practical. The desired aim is to be able to trust someone 100% for 100% of the time.

CHAPTER SIX

COMMAND, LEADERSHIP AND MANAGEMENT

Leadership is distinct from command and distinct from management. Command is the authority vested in an individual of the armed forces for the direction, coordination and control of military forces. It is the authority earned by rank, position, experience or expertise, which puts an individual in charge of what happens. In distinction, management is the ability to achieve objectives with the resources available (human, material, financial, time); and good managers apply the functions necessary to achieve their aim.

In the Royal Navy, management amounts to the ability of commanders to analyse, organise and execute decisions, and to control activity. Command is the power, management the science, and leadership the art needed in order to get things done.

Command, leadership and management are of course closely inter-related. The skills and competences required of each are broadly complementary and some are overlapping. Command provides the institutional authority. Leadership requires qualities such as professional judgement, intelligence and knowledge; yet these qualities must work alongside moral and personal qualities such as integrity, empathy, willpower, courage and confidence. In contrast, management functions tend to include planning, organising, controlling, coordinating, supporting, communicating and evaluating. In making these distinctions it is important to note that any one situation in the Royal Navy will draw on elements of command, leadership and management. But command and management, without good leadership, will not get things done.

1. **Command:** this is the position of authority and responsibility to which military staff are legally appointed. Leadership and management are the key components in the successful exercise of command.

2. **Leadership:** this is visionary; it is the projection of personality and character to inspire people to achieve a desired outcome. There is no prescription for leadership and no prescribed style of leader, though it can be recognised through a set of behaviours. Leadership is a combination of example, persuasion and compulsion and is dependent on the situation.

3. **Management:** this primarily concerns the allocation and control of resources (human, material and financial) to achieve objectives.

In practical terms there are differences in how command, leadership and management can be used to think about, match up, interact and create success. The table below sets out a range of behaviours or competencies, which are appropriate for each activity:

Competency	Command	Leadership	Management
Thinking	Clarifying superior intent	Setting the direction	Planning and Budgeting
Matching up	Ensuring subordinates' ability to meet remit	Aligning people to the task	Organising and staffing
Interact	Timely Decision Making	Motivating and Inspiring	Coordination and Problem Solving
Create Success	Success through determination	Mastery of the Context	Control of the Environment

This range of behaviours or competencies makes up a widening set of skills acquired through training and learning. The table below shows that more senior leaders will tend to have those skills set out in the upper third, whereas senior and junior managers will tend to have those skills set out in the lower two thirds:

	Conceptual	Aligning	Interactive	Create Success
Senior Leaders	Pragmatic Vision	Nor Risk Adverse Professionalism	Able to communicate effectively	Self-Belief
Senior Managers	Perspective	Integrity Reliability	Interpersonal sensitivity Influence	Delivers success Resilient
	Critical Analysis & Judgement	Organised Conscientious Empowering	Inspirational Motivating Persuasive	Committed Motivated
Junior Managers	Effective Intellect	Subordinate Development	Caring	Vigorous

Each level of skill is a necessary and sufficient qualification for the next level up. A senior manager should have all the skills of a junior manager and be developing the skills of a senior leader.

Ultimately, all leadership is to do with people. At every level, therefore, leadership can be distilled into a set of behaviours. These behaviours are the best way to handle relationships, convey the differences between command, leadership and management, and ensure that all three elements form part of getting things done.

At all times, however, getting things done requires not only the understanding of how command, leadership and management interact, but also a clear sense of how to motivate others. Irrespective of leadership style, the following are necessary to leading, inspiring and motivating a team:

- Promote the Six Core Values –Commitment, Courage, Discipline, Respect, Integrity and Loyalty
- Demonstrate the Twelve Leadership Qualities
- Engender commitment through enthusiasm
- Lead by example
- Display Naval ethos
- Demonstrate integrity and honesty
- Build esprit de corps
- Engender fighting spirit
- Agree targets to recognise achievement
- Delegate appropriately
- Develop individuals
- Regularly review performance and progress
- Reward successful performance

Because leadership deals with individuals and groups (sometimes quite large groups), the fundamentals of leadership govern relations between people. Any working definition of leadership, or set of guiding principles, therefore must attend to those relations. Leadership is above all a set of behaviours, which govern how one person relates to another: it is not something done *to* people but something done *with* them.

Command, leadership and management training takes place within the Divisional System – or structure – that exists for the all-round professional and moral welfare of the men and women of the Royal Navy. It is usually based on the chain of command.

CPO Billy May (surface fleet) Chief Physical Trainer, HMS ILLUSTRIOUS

There is no rank in sport. The best footballer on the park might be the youngest Rating. He might have a couple of Officers, couple of Senior Ratings playing on his side. But if he's the star footballer and he leads it doesn't matter what rank he is; the rest of the lads will follow him; because he leads, they follow. Being the expert is vital. There's a time and a place when one man will take charge of a situation because he may be the subject-matter expert. There might be six people left after an explosion and he might be the most junior rank there amongst the Senior Ratings and the Officers; but if he's the subject matter expert, and he puts his hand up and decides to lead, then you listen to what the subject-matter expert says. Rank, within reason, goes out of the window if you've got somebody that's a specialist.

THE DIVISIONAL SYSTEM

Every organisation or ship's company is divided into groups of about twenty under the authority of a Divisional Officer (or Divisional Senior Rating) who is charged with their professional and personal welfare. The Divisional System provides the structure within which a ship or establishment supervises, develops and trains the members of its company. It is the keystone of effective personnel management in the Royal Navy.

The Divisional System is therefore all about effectiveness in war fighting through efficiency, morale and welfare. It provides the structure to achieve that aim. At the same time, the system provides a framework that can address the general welfare of that company.

Informally, the Divisional structure can be thought of as 'family in the workplace'. A Divisional Officer's primary task is to command, lead, manage and look after their people, but this cannot be achieved successfully unless they know them. Knowledge of others is essential in understanding their particular and various needs for professional and personal support and development.

The Divisional System is the means by which work is evaluated and individuals are appraised, recommended for promotion, or selected for further training. It is the means by which sports, adventurous training, and other forms of recreation are promoted for the well-being of servicemen and women. It is also where the Navy's formal expertise on fairness, discipline, diversity, equality, conduct, complaints, allowances and other legal matters resides.

The Divisional System works by passing information – both formally and informally – up and down the chain of command. It is therefore a channel for management and leadership. As such, the principles of good leadership apply within the many conversations and relationships of the Divisional System. At the heart of Divisional responsibilities for all leaders are moral and pastoral care: the system exists for the good of the men and women within it. Leadership and the demonstration of leadership qualities are fundamental to that care, and Divisional responsibilities are taken seriously.

The primary role of all in authority in the Royal Navy is to offer leadership. Senior Ratings are a vital link in the chain that connects the Commanding Officer with his or her most junior sailor. Senior Ratings are involved in Divisional management and daily running of the Division. To this end, they are trained in Divisional responsibilities as part of the Senior Ratings Leadership Course (obligatory for all men and women selected for promotion to Petty Officer). The Divisional System in this way is completely integrated into the departmental structure on board a ship or submarine, or in a Royal Naval establishment. It is a highly flexible structure, extremely robust (over 250 years old), and sensitive to changes in technology and culture.

MARITIME THROUGH CAREER DEVELOPMENT

The Maritime Through Career Development framework considers Command Leadership and Management training over time, and suggests that the skills required will change from the early task-centred leadership to a more strategic approach later in an individual's career. This framework allows leadership training packages to be set against the differing requirement at different career stages:

CLM:	Warfare Specific	Education
IOT – Initial Officer Training	**IWOC** – Initial Warfare Officers Course	**IMWarC** – Intermediate Maritime Warfare Course
JOLC – Junior Officers Leadership Course 1	**FNO** – Frigate Navigating Officers Course **MWO** – Mine Warfare Officer **MCDO** – Mine Clearance Diving Officer (Course) **FC** – Fighter Controller	**MWarC** – Maritime Warfare Course
DOC – Divisional Officers Course		
JOLC2 – Junior Officers Leadership Course 2		
ICSC – Initial Command and Staff Course (Maritime)		
ACSC – Advanced Command and Staff Course	**PWO** – Principal Warfare Officer	
HCSC – Higher Command and Staff Course	**AWO** – Advanced Warfare Officer **A** – Air **U** - Underwater **C** – Communications **N** – Navigation	
RCDS – Royal College of Defence Studies	**XODC** – Executive Officer (Designated) Course	
DSLP – Defence Strategic Leadership Programme	**CODC** – Commanding Officer (Designated) Course	

Maritime through career development

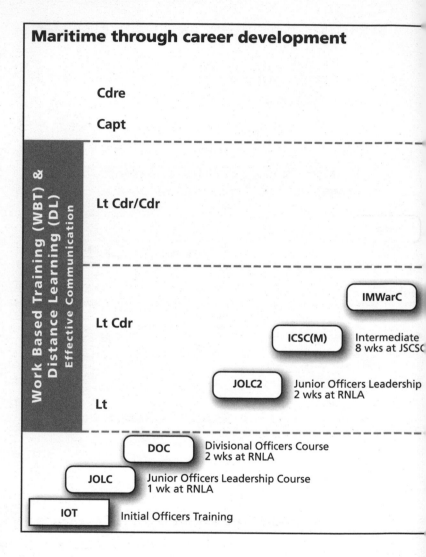

Cdre

Capt

Work Based Training (WBT) & Distance Learning (DL)
Effective Communication

Lt Cdr/Cdr

Lt Cdr

IMWarC

ICSC(M) — Intermediate 8 wks at JSCSC

JOLC2 — Junior Officers Leadership 2 wks at RNLA

Lt

DOC — Divisional Officers Course 2 wks at RNLA

JOLC — Junior Officers Leadership Course 1 wk at RNLA

IOT — Initial Officers Training

DSLP

RCDS

HCSC

Stage 4 – Higher

ACSC Advanced Command and Staff Course

MWarC Maritime Warfare Course
3 wks at MWC Course

Stage 3 – Advanced

Initial Maritime Warfare Course
1 wk at MWC Course

Command and Staff Course (Maritime)

Course 2

Stage 2 – Intermediate

Stage 1 – Initial
Initial Core Maritime Skills Development

Continuation Core Maritime Skills Development

For example, this is what the leadership training for a warfare specialist would be:

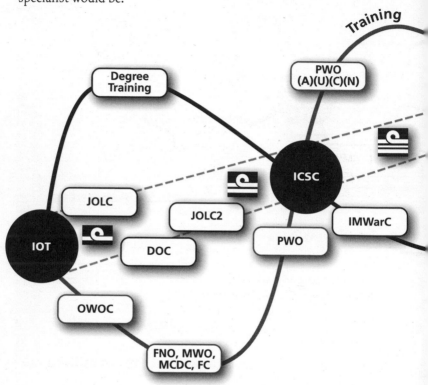

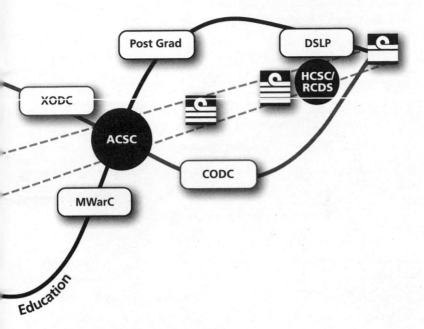

LEADERSHIP THINKING

The theoretical basis of leadership training delivered by the RNLA is twofold; Action Centred Leadership (ACL) and Situational Leadership. By means of theoretical instruction and practical training and assessment the courses develop command, leadership and management skills. These include training in the theory of leadership; motivation and morale; power, authority and influence within groups; planning, briefing and communications; evaluation and measurement of the outcome of an event.

Lt Sarah Clewes RN Logistics Officer, HMS ARGYLL

Having served for 14 years as a rating before passing out
as an Officer from Britannia Royal Naval College in 2005,
the continual exposure to Naval Command Leadership and
Management, underpinned by the doctrine that applies from
Leading Hand to 1*, has enabled me to develop my individual
leadership style. This, together with application of recognised
taught leadership models, has negated any potential issues
within the mix of a team; the leader is always at the forefront
and irrefutably in charge.

Action Centred (or Functional) Leadership, distilled into a Venn
diagram by John Adair, is the first leadership theory taught in the
Royal Navy. The idea is that a leader must consider and balance the
task in hand, the strength of the team and the needs of the individual.

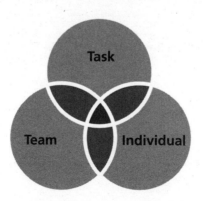

Along with this powerful way of thinking about the task, the team and the role of the individual, there is a seven-point checklist:

Thinking

1. Ask yourself: What is the task? What resources do I have? What is my plan? How can it best be achieved?

Acting

2. Explain the task: clearly brief the team; check their understanding.

3. Plan Solution: give your *own* solution; encourage suggestions and skills; decide on the *best* solution.

4. Deploy: brief the team on the final plan; and set timings and targets; delegate tasks giving precise instructions; set the team to work giving them the tools for the job; try to involve everyone.

5. Monitor and Support: coordinate activities; assist and advise where necessary; keep everyone informed and updated.

6. Assess Progress: check that standards and targets are being achieved; make adjustments, if necessary, and keep the team informed.

Debriefing

7. Check that the task is completed; give an accurate debrief honestly assessing strengths and weaknesses.

This reliable, straightforward action-centred approach underpins both the Leading Ratings Leadership Course and Initial Officers Training.

Other common-sense approaches to leadership account for more variables: the situation and its urgency or importance; the capability of the team and the individuals in it; the kinds of professional expertise available.

In practice, no single style suits all occasions; effective leadership occurs when the right leadership style is matched to an individual's (or team's) level of development in a particular task. This approach produces a range of leadership behaviours – from directing to coaching to supporting to delegating– which match the increasing competence and commitment of the individual being led. Above all, there is the need to be flexible, to acknowledge that the most important situational variable in leadership is the developmental needs of the subordinate. This idea also supports the Royal Navy's commitment to developing subordinates to be self-reliant and proactive in the workplace.

It does so by means of directing, coaching, supporting and delegating; these sit on a sliding scale. Some tasks require direct intervention, others a more democratic approach. There are many such models in leadership thinking, but the general idea behind them all is that the leader is autocratic at one extreme and democratic at the other. The flexibility of the Royal Navy approach is that it accounts for the complexities and subtleties of any situation (importance, urgency, tactical or strategic) and the overall context.

Aside from the formal instruction and assessment, the following skills and qualities are essential and are learned at all levels rather than overtly taught. These are:

1. **Resilience**: both mental and physical. The latter is particularly important in the physically arduous stages of leadership training and includes the ability to manage under conditions of little sleep and adverse weather. Another word for this is Grit: simply put, the ability to overcome cold, fatigue and sleep deprivation on the one hand and sudden changes and uncertainty on the other.

2. **Planning and presentation**: the planning and briefing process (Seven Questions and NATO Sequence of Orders) is fundamental, particularly under stressful conditions. Fluency, clarity and brevity in presentation; accuracy and flexibility in briefing; agility and speed of execution are all vital.

3. **Delegation**: this is fundamental to success on the course; on-the-spot thinking (particularly in 'leaderless tasks') is of great value.

Those who are successful on their professional leadership courses develop an ability to set tasks in priority (or prioritise), to keep things simple, to ask questions, to listen. They rely on their team and recognise that colleagues can do more than they think while at the same time making allowances for weaknesses or tiredness; they prepare for a range of eventualities; and they develop self-confidence in the team and in themselves.

Lt Maxine Kim Ashby RN DLO, HMS OCEAN

Leadership at all levels within the Royal Navy is a fundamental part of our everyday work environment that we take for granted, be it our own or that of our subordinates, peers and superiors. The ability to learn from experience, combined with personal development, is vital if as leaders we expect to gain the respect and co-operation of others in any given situation. The importance of 'good' leadership should not be underestimated and is an ongoing programme of personal development, which will ensure that all personnel achieve their best and have the opportunity to learn and develop themselves.

COACHING AND MENTORING

In a military organisation, promotion generally comes from within. Shaping successors is part of command, leadership and management. As part of this effort, coaching plays a vital role. Coaching demonstrates that the Royal Navy values its people as individuals. It offers ways of developing leaders through analysis, reflection and action plans. It must be carried out within an atmosphere of trust and confidence so that individuals can speak freely. By being encouraged to break the mould of current thinking and learning to cope with critical feedback, an individual is able to reflect on his or her attitudes and in doing so has the opportunity for self-knowledge. A coach stimulates effective feedback through effective questioning, creating a learning environment. The Naval Service seeks to exploit this approach.

Train – Instruct – Coach – Mentor – Direct

Coaching sits on a spectrum of relationships; at one end, the behaviour is autocratic; at the other, democratic. Most coaching relationships take place somewhere between the two extremes. Coaching represents a particular engagement with an individual in order to help that individual achieve a specific goal. That goal might be success in a task; or it might be a change in behaviour. Coaching does not provide solutions; it helps with clarity. The answer lies within the individual; what a coach does, through question, answer, and discussion, is to find the answer that an individual knows is there. The coach facilitates clarity of thought.

Col Jim Hutton RM (Royal Marines) Director of Training, CTCRM Lympstone

A coach helps with clarity. Coaching, mentoring and training are all related. Coaching relies on the individual. Coaching is not mentoring and it's not training. Coaches do not provide solutions. The solution to your issue lies within you; what I do, through question and answer and discussion with you, is help you find the answer that you know is in there. You just don't want to admit it; or the thought of doing it is so horrendous you push it to one side, but you really know, deep down, what it is. And so what the coach will do is facilitate that clarity of thought.

The use of coaching ensures that all personnel perform to their maximum potential. It is a central part of MTCD and is vital to the teaching and learning of leadership. Coaching keeps people motivated and capable in their work; coaching promotes the Six Core Values and Twelve Leadership Qualities and can aid the retention of personnel.

The use of coaching marks a change in how the Royal Navy develops teams; coaching may take longer than the traditional

'Tell' style because there is a marked increase in responsibility and ownership of the issue through the 'Ask' approach of coaching. The 'Tell' style clearly has its place in a disciplined service, but the 'Ask' style encourages each individual to learn and to take responsibility for his or her own development.

In essence, coaching is the art of releasing the potential in another in order to improve performance. The coach need not be an expert in the subject area but must have credibility in the eyes of the coachee in order to build the relationship. The coach uses a non-leading approach within a structured conversation, asking non-leading questions and actively listening in order to understand the coachee's perspective. There are four elements:

1. Following the coachee's interest: by allowing the coachee to set the agenda, it is more likely that the coachee will be motivated to address the issue seriously;
2. Raising awareness: the coach allows the coachee to develop a new insight into and awareness of the issue;
3. Removing interference: the coach promotes focus and clarity
4. Leaving choice with the coachee: the performance of a coachee will not change unless they choose to do something differently.

Coaching has boundaries. Leaders often find themselves coaching, mentoring and training; it is dependent on the circumstances.

Moreover, the way a coach deals with an AB or a Marine will be dependent on the situation and the task in hand. Teaching, coaching and mentoring are matched to the environment.

The Royal Navy recommends two main techniques for coaching; the widely known GROW model (reproduced below, adapted from John Whitmore), combined with Effective Debriefing and Feedback.

WRAP-UP

Clarity

Support

GOAL

For session

OPTIONS

What is possible

REALITY

Who – What – Where – How – When

Effective Debriefing and Feedback is essentially a way of thinking, questioning and careful listening designed to encourage personnel to assess their own performance. Effective Debriefing will ask rather than tell, using open questions such as 'What went well?'; 'What didn't go as well as you would have liked?' and 'What can you do differently next time?'

Mentoring, in contrast to coaching, is a process where a more experienced person supports another's development outside the normal command structure. The mentor offers insights based on experience and wisdom, usually during a longer-term relationship. Mentors tend to be older and more senior than those they guide. Mentors will often have been along the same path as those they mentor. Effective mentors offer counsel on development needs and allow their mentees to explore their own solutions to the problems they face.

Used in conjunction with coaching, Mentoring helps people to achieve their maximum potential and is a key link in promoting emotional intelligence. On a larger scale, a good coaching and mentoring programme – such as the one followed by the Royal Navy and Royal Marines – is evidence of an organisation that learns collectively and has a rich shared intelligence.

CHAPTER SEVEN

LEADERSHIP IN THE FUTURE

Col Jim Hutton RM (Royal Marines) Director of
Training, CTCRM Lympstone

If you could summarise everything you learn and put it into
three words your aide memoir, the catch phrase, when it's
all going to hell in a hand basket, what do you need to do?
'Listen. Decide. Learn.' The three things a leader needs to
do. First of all, listen. Listen to the advice you're getting, and
listen in terms of what you're reading, i.e. the information
you're getting. Decide. Make a decision – because that's what
leaders do. And then learn.

The trends in international security likely to have an impact on leaders
fall broadly into globalisation, climate change and global inequality.
The commercial equivalents of these are fourfold: first, a shift in global
economic activity from developed to developing economies; second,
a growth in the number of consumers in emerging markets; third,
technologies that enable a free flow of information worldwide; and
fourth, increasingly global labour markets. Finally, current thinking

on climate change, population and energy predicts that by 2030 the world will need 50% more food, 50% more energy and 30% more water than in 2010.

In leadership terms what flows from an overall appreciation of any strategic context is the ability to form a series of plans. This process in essence is the same as a Combat Estimate or Maritime Estimate, although the information required is more diverse (but not necessarily more complex) and has several stages:

1.   Diplomatic, Military and Economic Analysis: information and a range of social and military intelligence is vital here;
2.   Mission Analysis: this sets the political intent and maps out the end state to support the strategic objectives in view;
3.   Strategic Centre of Gravity Analysis: this sets out the critical requirements, capabilities and vulnerabilities in terms of time, place and resources;
4.   Planning Considerations: lines of operation, sequences and phases, branches and sequels, pauses and culmination;
5.   Courses of Action: costs, benefits, risks.

Leadership at a strategic level, in war and in peace, involves taking decisions about the future direction of a military organisation when few issues are clear cut. It is the leader's role to bring clarity, persuade others of his or her vision, and to communicate persuasively with government, industry, the media and the general public; other foreign military and governments, international organisations such as the European Union, United Nations, NATO, relief organisations and NGOs may also at times form part of the strategic leader's constituency of interest. The strategic leader must answer four fundamental questions:

1. What is the ultimate objective (the end)?
2. What means are available (the resources)?
3. Do the means enable the way (the strategy)?
4. As circumstances alter, is there a better way?

By answering these, the strategic leader can form his or her intent. The emphasis is on the flexibility, agility and resilience of the thinking.

The following trends in international security will shape the challenges for the next generation of leaders. These challenges will not necessarily mean that leadership styles will change; but they do require that a flexible combination of expertise be applied:

1. Disputes over water will contribute to tensions in volatile regions.
2. Exceptional nuclear-armed states will remain vulnerable to instability.

3. Terrorism motivated by religion will persist.

4. Irregular activity will be prevalent.

5. Soft Power (the ability to use it and resist it) will be of importance to states and non-states.

6. Affordable technology will benefit the less technologically capable.

7. Transitional knowledge-sharing and innovation will expand.

8. Armed forces in low-income nations will operate alongside and against parliamentary groups and armed criminals.

9. All likely future opponents will have recognised the advantages of 'going underground', especially in complex urban spaces.

The following trends will probably have an influence:

1. Mass population displacement may be the result of climate change, pressure on resources and economic advantage.

2. Military forces may become more involved in humanitarian commitments.

3. Security – and scarcity – of national resources may necessitate the use of military intervention.

4. The risks associated with failing states and ungoverned spaces may increase.

5. Trans-national, inter-communal conflict may increase.

This set of circumstances means that future conflict environments (subject to pervasive media and Internet coverage) will pose a significant challenge to armed forces operating in them.

These environments will require new tactics, specialised equipment and heightened levels of discrimination. All military personnel will require an increased awareness of the legal and cultural implications of their actions; this must be supported by sophisticated training based on objective doctrine. A wider range of skills will be needed for the command and deployment of agile, effective forces.

The leadership and command skills required are not necessarily part of the current UK military outlook. The future appears to take the form of short-notice amphibious operations leading to complex, fast-moving, fluctuating and difficult coastal and urban environments. This has an impact on the Royal Navy's capacity to train its men and women before they are deployed.

The UK's High Level Operational Concept for joint UK operations and capabilities over the next twenty years recognises the likelihood that in addition to major combat operations, the protection of UK interests may demand military intervention on a short-term expeditionary basis. There is a realisation that stabilisation operations (and joint operations with international allies) and conflict with irregular enemies (i.e., war amongst the people), can be more challenging than major combat operations.

In recent operations, the enemy is multifarious, concealed and unaccountable; the civilian population – the key to these conflicts – is of mixed loyalty, different culture, complex nature and may well contain numbers of the enemy. Relations with allies, host-nation security and its government and local representatives are complex and shifting. Military operations are pursued before a sceptical global media, a domestic audience, many interested NGOs and under international legal scrutiny.

It is essential that leaders currently in training (one of whom may well be at commanding officer level by 2030), have a clear grasp of the future operating environment and its complexities. Leadership in the future will, of course, include those principles that are set out in this book; it will also include greater competence in the following areas:

1. An understanding of influence and constituencies and their relation to tactical planning and fighting.
2. An understanding that information flows upwards from the battle space.
3. Awareness of culture and diversity.
4. Communication skills.
5. An understanding and appreciation of joint, inter-agency and multi-national operations.
6. Command and control remain vital, but there are challenges for leaders as new technology allows them to work remotely.

7.   Dispersed decision-making.

8.   Improvisation.

Leaders in the future will have to be adept at handling fast-moving and complex environments, have a clear sense of the intricacies of modern conflict, and the confidence to think and act with clarity.

CHAPTER EIGHT

INSIGHTS

The Core Values and Twelve Leadership Qualities express themselves personally in each individual. The mix and expression of these qualities depends on the individual's character, on the operational context, and on the members of the team; and there may be other variables, of course. What follows is a set of insights on the Navy's Six Core Values and Twelve Leadership Qualities. Clearly there is a tight relationship between core values and leadership qualities (integrity, moral courage and trust are common to both sets). There is ample latitude in the Navy's values to allow for individual interpretation of universally understood values: how a particular person acts at a given time and place. These insights show the variety of opinion consistent with those values.

These insights recognise that everyone does his or her job differently. The views expressed here are individual insights, not necessarily endorsed by the Naval Service. They are the result of many hours of interviews across the Royal Navy: on training, operations, deployment, in all types of craft and on land, at sea, and in the air. For ease of reference they are grouped under Core Values and Leadership

Qualities. These insights should form a basis for discussion and offer distilled personal experience of leading men and women in the Naval Service; they are included here to allow the reader to reflect on a range of observations as he or she evolves a particular style.

INSIGHTS ON THE SIX CORE VALUES

Commitment

Maj Andy Lock RM (Royal Marines) Command Wing, CTCRM Lympstone

It's easy for me, even as a Company Commander, to share the same experiences as my men in Afghanistan because I'm in the same place when the RPGs [rocket propelled grenades] are landing around us I'm going through the same experiences. So when that RPG lands and – as they do – the guys look to you, the question is: 'What are we going to do now?' You get that 'Private Ryan' moment all the time. 'How are we going to deal with this?' I'm as scared as the young Marine lying next to me, or wherever we are. But of course you've got so much to think about you have to take stock of yourself. You certainly never ever show any fear because that's the worst thing you can possibly do; and then you crack on and deal with it.

On a ship matters can be different. People are separated into different Departments. If you're working in the Engine Room, you're probably never going to see how effective and committed an Operations Officer is; so how do you get over that? How do you bring people together across departments? The easy solution is sport, PT, Adventurous Training.

Courage

Lt Cdr Tim Wright RN (surface fleet) Officer Commanding Initial Officer Training, BRNC Dartmouth

My mission is to deliver courageous leaders with the spirit to fight and win. I'm not trying to create a specialist. I want them to have the basics of leadership and officership. I don't want to produce carbon copies of a particular style of leadership because it's got to be commensurate with personality, which is why I like my staff to have a variety of styles.

The one thing that will mark out a successful leader is the ability to judge the situation and work out what is appropriate and when; and then how to do it. The judgement element is incredibly important, almost impossible to teach because there is no formula: there is no one way of doing it. Anything that focuses the mind and makes people think about leadership and their own style of leadership, how they would perform in certain scenarios, is hugely beneficial.

Discipline

PO Bruce Milne (surface fleet) HMS ILLUSTRIOUS

This is a disciplined service, morally and professionally. Everybody learns every day. You add to your professional capacity. There has to be a level of professional pride. I'd never let mine dip, and nor would I let anybody dip beneath it if they're in my vicinity. I delegate a lot. I tell the person what the job is, what the task entails, any safety equipment they've got to take, and then: 'Do you fully understand the task that I've set you?' You're openly asking them to ask you questions back. I expect them to act in a disciplined and self-disciplined way.

My way of leadership is to be approachable to the lads; they can come to me with anything. When I speak they listen to me because I pitch the level right. We've got all sorts from sixteen-year olds, up to people in their fifties on board; you've got to know where your happy medium is.

Respect

Lt Col Jeremy Burnell RM (Royal Marines) Force Protection
Group Royal Marines (FPGRM)

Regardless of rank all of us in the Marines have gone through training
at Lympstone. One of the strongest themes for me as a Royal
Marines officer is the fact that we have this kind of shared respect.

There is an informed respect because we all know the process;
it is a bond that people admire. Why is that? What is it about Royal
Marines that make them do that? It's their sense of independence,
their sense of self-worth, their persistence and determination to
succeed and never to be thwarted. We're not the types who just say,
'Can't do this.'

Integrity

Lt Hugo Sedgwick RN (submarine fleet) HMS TRENCHANT

Leadership means taking responsibility for making sure things are
done in the first place, having the clear presence of mind of knowing
when they need to be done sufficiently early, and selecting people to
do them. It contains all the nuances of what management does, but
grows into something slightly more. You have to have the personal
integrity to take responsibility of what you're in charge of.

Leadership is inspiring someone through something which would be hard work and perhaps unfamiliar to them. Leadership is bringing people on that extra bit beyond what they normally expect to do. On a submarine people expect to do things intuitively because they've done them many times or they've trained for something many times. Here I see leadership as a way of motivating people who might be flagging or whose focus might be drifting.

Loyalty

Lt Cdr Russ Haines RN (surface fleet) Officer Commanding, RNLA COLLINGWOOD

Loyalty means different things to different people. For most, loyalty will be tested at some point in their lives and it is vital that we understand how to deal with it and consider what the consequences might be. But we all experience it. Loyalty underpins the very nature of what we do in the Naval Service.

It is ingrained when you first join the Navy; loyalty to your new entry classmates who are all experiencing the same emotions when you first leave home; loyalty to your branch or trade when you complete your professional training; loyalty to your new messmates when you join your first ship and to the ship itself. The longer you serve the more that loyalty becomes instilled within you and is something that grows as you progress. Ultimately it's all about personal pride, both in wearing the uniform and in telling people about what you do, but also about how you conduct yourself in your everyday life. It's also important to recognise that loyalty goes both ways; everyone should expect to display it from the upper ranks down to the most junior sailor, even if sometimes we may question it. Both individually and as a team, it is vital that we get it right.

INSIGHTS ON TWELVE LEADERSHIP QUALITIES

1. Capacity for judgement and decision making

Rear Admiral Mark Anderson (submarine fleet)
Commander of Operations

Particularly as a submarine commander, but in any leadership sense, when something goes wrong, there is a moment's silence. Everyone turns to look at you. They're not necessarily expecting you to issue the order that's going to make it all right. They're looking at you to measure whether they're OK or not, whether there is confidence in your demeanour. You do have to develop – even though inside you can be paddling like hell – rather a stoic outer manner.

And I did develop that in submarines and in ships as well so that I am not seen to be flustered. I can continue to be relaxed and stoic; otherwise the organisation underneath me will stop and worry, 'Why is the Captain looking worried?' rather than continuing. There is an element of acting which needs to be ingrained in your character; you can't pretend.

Lt Cdr John Gray RN (submarine fleet) XO,
HMS VENGEANCE

If you need to make a decision you make it and you take the consequences. That's what being in command is, isn't it? If you've got time you don't make a rash decision, a decision based on scant information, because you've got the time to get more information. So the process of decision making is time-line dependent.

The worst thing I can be is not confident because if I lose the confidence of my crew the whole performance becomes based on nerves; and the last thing a commanding officer needs to lose is the confidence of his crew. So if you're confident in your decision making you say, 'Right. Let's do this.' But if it goes wrong you say, 'That didn't work. Let's try this.' And there's no element of regret.

If your decision is required in ten minutes, you've got ten minutes' worth of information gathering; you make the decision in ten minutes. If it's an instant decision, you base it on what you know, on your experience. But rash decisions inherently don't work unless you're lucky all the time. Decisions need to be based on as much information as you can gather in the time that you've got. And in a submarine you generally don't have a great deal of time because you're working in three dimensions.

For example, on board a ship I would quickly find out whether or not my leadership style/man management style would work, and then I would adapt. I find that a calm, controlled, professional non-aggressive way gets results; and that's because of the elitism in the man I'm trying to motivate.

Cdr Stephen Mackay RN (surface fleet) Commander

Fighting at sea is all about leadership, not about management. When you are fighting the ship from the Ops Room information is precious; you are on it like a flash, making decisions, handling the movements of ships and aircraft. That is leadership.

When you're in trouble at sea it becomes crystal clear very quickly who's in charge; and with a Captain, it's always the Captain. That's where the buck stops.

Now when you're managing the thing and not actually being a passionate part of it, it's quiet, because there's not much information going on, people are keeping their heads down: 'That's not my job, that's his job', and the whole thing runs completely differently. You don't get things done. It looks as though it's okay, but it isn't. To make the team work, you definitely need leadership of people, not management of resources, assets, or anything else.

Lt James Shortall RN (surface fleet) HMS ILLUSTRIOUS

You evaluate yourself; you're forced to. You're always evaluating yourself and others, but the way that you bring these qualities out is through experience and just doing. And that's why the Practical Leadership Tasks – the PLTs – are so important, because until you get out there and stand in front of a group of people and the decisions are yours, you won't know what it's like … that feeling of being slightly out of control.

And that happens in training for all levels and all ranks. It happens in the simulator for submarine captains on Perisher Course, it happens to navigators, captains, and ABs. You're completely out of your comfort zone. Panic can set in and freeze you. It freezes your thoughts and your ability to think clearly and to make a decision, any decision.

Good leaders can widen the field of vision: it's all about feeling 'spare capacity'. And building 'spare capacity' means that someone can throw something completely new in, a real shock, and you'll be able to deal with it. At the start, for everybody it's the same. You're only really able to just follow things through in the order that you've been set to do; but you get better, develop a bit of potential to deal with other things. That is just what the training achieves.

'What do we do?' That question is pertinent to everybody who leads to whatever level, whether they're sitting on the Navy Board or on a quarter-deck when things are starting to go wrong. 'What do we do?' You still have to have a grasp of what it is that needs doing, the overall aim, and how best you can achieve it.

2. Cheerfulness

Capt Will Northcott RM (Royal Marines) Training Command Wing, CTCRM Lympstone

Being able to make the uncertain certain is the secret to leadership. There are times when you have to be careful with this because you can't be economical with the truth; and there are times when you have to be the personification of optimism. However bad things get and however concerned you are, inwardly, you must always be the picture of optimism.

But equally you also have to understand that if you are always über-optimistic about everything then the effect of your optimism, over time, is reduced. If you are always utterly optimistic in every single situation you can actually start to have the opposite effect.

A good leader can handle uncertainty and must be able to

command in an uncertain situation. In other words, you've got a whole troop, and no one knows what the hell's going on; in that situation you're as uncertain as they are about what's going to happen but you have still got the leadership to be able to keep them going and prevent them from giving up.

Lt George Storton RN (surface fleet) CO, HMS PUNCHER

I'm a strong believer in team work and I'll always push at my team, just occasionally nipping on to the bridge and saying, 'Look, you've been up here a couple of hours, do you want a cup of coffee?' and doing things like that, really driving them forward. And the biggest thing I've found in building that team is doing briefs for the team. Every time we get alongside we get all my bridge team together, we go straight to the bridge and sit down to talk about what happened this week, what's going to happen next week, get them involved in the planning side.

It is a team effort with me the focal point in all the command matters. And that's something I've developed recently and it works. It's about trying to find that way to pull your team together, get the ideas from them, and draw from them what's going on and, to a certain extent, fight their case as well. If you're cheerful, used to being light about things, you also send another message out about confidence and capability.

3. Clarity and vision

Admiral Sir James Burnell-Nugent (submarine fleet)
Second Sea Lord and Chief of Naval Home Command
(2003–05)

I love simplicity. But we know the world is complex, of course.
Obviously there's a relationship between complexity and chaos.
But again, I think that maybe I'm helped slightly by being a
mathematician. So personally I find it fairly easy to break down
complexity into simplicity. I'm certainly intimidated by complexity,
but I think that the way to tackle complexity is to simplify it every
time. As for ambiguity, you mustn't allow it to happen. And in
any statement of intent a whiff of ambiguity will undermine your
position and the clarity of your leadership; people will see you're
sitting on the fence and that's not good. But more worryingly,
ambiguity will dissipate efforts, because at least half your people will
be pursuing the wrong objective.

Lt Cdr Stuart 'Sharky' Finn RN (fleet air arm) 771 NAS

'Have you done your command estimate?' I'm a great believer in
Mission Command. When the call comes in we're airborne routinely
within less than ten minutes, airborne off to a rescue. We don't know
what we're going to when the call comes, so these different scenarios

and 'what ifs' go through your mind and the plan has to be there. We allow for these by means of the Flying Estimate.

So you have to formulate a plan and you have to think about all the different scenarios and the 'what ifs': weather, sea state, or where are we going to take this person? What happens if we get out there and we can't do this? There's a lot to process in a short space of time.

I have to trust my commanders to do the mission, regardless. They do not need to speak to anybody; it's a decision that they make on their own. That is Mission Command at work. So there's a high level of responsibility and trust that I bestow upon them. There's not one person here – because they wouldn't have that authorisation – I don't trust. In the aircraft everyone trusts everyone. It has to be that way. A crew is a family; you are as one.

4. Communication skills

WO1 Russ Billings (surface fleet) EWO, HMS ILLUSTRIOUS

Talk to people. It's fundamental. And listen to them. Just sitting down and allowing someone to talk, giving someone two minutes of your time is key. And regardless of whether it's an Officer, a Senior Rating or a Junior Rating, I can take so much away from the little things they've said. As a manager you need to continuously talk and understand; but don't listen to negatives, promote positives. You've got to remain positive and focused. Promote the organisation and don't deviate or you lose your grasp on how to manage your people.

Communication is essential from baseline to end state. Whether that's for a short-term task or a long-term process doesn't matter. And the start of that communication link, when you provide information to the different levels of management, is vital because it sets the standard. From communication comes direction. Anyone will do a job for you if they're directed properly.

Lt Cdr Colin Nicklas RN (surface fleet) OC, RNLA

There is an established link between communication and leadership. And there is, undoubtedly, a link between confidence and leadership. People who are more confident generally are better leaders. Those who suffer with low self-confidence, low self-esteem, perhaps are not so good unless they can find a coping mechanism.

In that context what is tested and tried is their performance as a leader, their ability to think straight, to do the problem-solving – the effective intelligence to analyse the problem and to find a solution – that comes from confidence in their own ability. Then they must be able to plan, again, linked to confidence and ability; to then brief the message and genuinely get the message across, not just the mechanics of it, but the inspiring bit of leadership, and that's all about powers of communication.

The power of communication, in the wider sense – including body language, the energy level, the use of the voice, all those sorts of things –not only helps get the detail across but also the 'buy-in'. Any officer can reel off a pre-prepared brief and give the information but if it's dull or monotone, with the wrong choice of words, wrong tone, wrong body language, they won't get their team to move and it will then become an ongoing struggle to complete the task. But if they do it right and they start to inspire their people to deliver.

Lt Cdr Rory West RN (surface fleet) XO, HMS ARGYLL

As the XO if I ask for something to be done it will generally be done. As a junior officer, for instance, you'd have to explain more; now I explain as a nicety and because it gets better results ultimately. But if something needs doing my direction will be sufficient to get it done. With that comes the responsibility of making sure what you're asking is a suitable and correct thing to be asking. In terms of leadership: put your plan across, take any comments, and then adjust the course as necessary; it works nicely.

My leadership now is wider. It is really making sure people are given the information to go away and do their own bits of leadership in making something happen. I explain everything that they will need to know making sure they go away with Mission Command, all the information they need to then achieve it. I check on completion.

5. Confidence

WO1 Neil Bennett (surface fleet) RNLA

'Right. Who's afraid of heights?' Somebody's fear is somebody
else's excitement; everybody gets something different. If you've got
somebody who can't read a map and they go out with snow falling, a
wind chill of -30, navigating from A to B, and they get around in six
hours without being lost, they come off the mountain with a sense
of achievement. Confidence comes from overcoming adversity, from
getting through.

These are stressful situations handled in a controlled way
where we can just see how people behave as leaders and also allow/
encourage/help them to push themselves and extend their capability.
Adventurous Training does bring a lot out of people by providing
stressful situations that replicate stress in the extremes of peacetime
or war.

Lt Cdr John Gray RN (submarine fleet) XO, HMS TRENCHANT

I haven't changed my character at all with respect to how I do
business. And that's what the Submarine Command Course does.
Decision making is a requirement of anybody in command; the
process by which that is achieved is by standing back, observing
overall, thinking about what's happened in the past ... i.e., falling

back on what experience you've got. If there's nothing in your pot of experience, then you give your best stab, in effect. If you don't know, just make a decision and be confident.

LH Victoria Hobby (surface fleet) Dental Nurse, HMS ILLUSTRIOUS

I do have a lot more confidence in myself. I've learnt so much especially doing the Duty Medic side. I have so much more confidence in First Aiding and teaching people as well. When I first started I didn't really know much myself and did not ask; but now I'm quite confident enough to say to somebody, 'How would you do this?'

Since being in the Navy I've probably got a longer fuse. I don't shout as much now. I just step back now and think; then I'll go back ten minutes later. I think a lot more about what I say before I actually say it.

Lt Cdr David Jones RN (submarine fleet) MEO, HMS TRENCHANT

The main quality is something that can be developed: self-confidence. To do anything, to impose yourself on any situation, you have to have confidence in your own abilities, your own judgement, your own assessments, and your professional knowledge of whatever's going on. That doesn't mean you have to be the expert on everything that's going on. I quite freely admit I don't know how all the kit works because I've got skilled technicians who are the experts on their bit of kit. My job's to bring it all together and provide it to command.

But it doesn't matter what job an officer can end up doing or what their branch is if they don't have self-confidence; then, effectively, they won't do anything. They'll react rather than trying to affect what's going on. I used to say when I was in basic leadership development, 'Mistakes aren't a problem. Everyone makes mistakes. Just try not to make the same one twice.' Learn from that.

Capt Philip Titterton RN (submarine fleet) JTEPS MOD Whitehall

The Navy does enduring operations all the time. It goes on deterrent patrols – that is an 'operation.' And the people doing those operations certainly feel that they are on operations. When do you recognise the seriousness of it all? The answer is, when something starts going wrong – for real. And it's right up until as late as that; it certainly was for me. For me it was my crew when we had a collision and the boat was sinking. And they all look at you, expecting the old man to pull something out of the bag.

Who knows what's going to happen next, at the time? So you get this moment when the boys will expect the man in charge to take some action that (1) keeps them alive and safe, and then (2) less so to them, but more so to you, does the mission. And if you don't take any action then you've lost it for the rest of the time. There's no way you can recover from that. When they needed you, you did not step up to the plate. That's it.

PO Richard Voller (surface fleet) SRCC student, RNLA

You've got to be up there with confidence because if you're talking to someone and they don't think you're confident, they're not going to have confidence in you to lead. You've got to have a certain aura, you've got to have command presence, to be able to speak and project your voice. A lot of this is psychological. It's all about command presence and asserting yourself. You can have the presence in a calm collected manner and probably even get the task done better and faster without screaming and shouting. You've got to know the people you work with. You've got to know your subordinates as well as the people above you, what they expect of you. You meet expectations by transferring urgency to your team.

6. Humanity and humility

LOM(C) Natasha Connerton (surface fleet) LOM(C), HMS ILLUSTRIOUS

You are the Officer given the opportunity to take charge of the watch. You want to speak to others as equals but also you don't want them to mess about with your watch; you want them to respect you for what you're doing. I just speak to people and treat them as I would like to be.

Capt Stephen Hart RM (Royal Marines) Command Wing, CTCRM Lympstone

The key quality is high emotional intelligence. I mean interpersonal skills. It is often said 'you don't need to be popular to be a leader. It's not a popularity contest.' But popularity helps. Clearly it depends how one defines popularity. People need to like you enough to follow you. They won't follow you if they hate you. And if people despise you they won't follow you effectively. You do need to be popular as a leader or rather your leadership needs to be popular, if not necessarily yourself as an individual.

The key personal quality is humility. You need to be humble and you need to have the capacity for learning which comes from humility. And if there is a quality I would say is pre-eminent over and above the others it would be humility because you need to be able to take on what other people are saying, to learn from your mistakes, and to have a capacity to apply that learning. There's no space for any arrogance in command. That said, you do see effective leaders who are arrogant.

Whether they agree with you in the round or whether they agree with you sufficiently to follow you is ultimately neither here nor there because the output is the same. So you need to have that confidence in yourself. You're right, but you must be humble. You must 'Serve to lead.' You have a responsibility up to your commander and you must make sure that your command decisions 'nest' inside the decisions of your higher commander.

I don't subscribe to the 'born leader' philosophy. Leadership is something you learn and develop. Some people never get it. Some people never have that capacity, but only a relatively small number. Most people can develop an understanding, although it's something that can't really be taught, it is an experience-based quality. It can be learned but it can't be taught.

Lt Cdr Cathy Lacey RN Sea Appointments

We lead and direct our sailors as a team and as a group of individuals, taking into account all their strengths and weaknesses and it was ever thus. As an Engineering Officer, the vast majority of my staff have always been male, but I have never perceived an issue with them having a female 'boss'. We are all judged on our professionalism, not on chromosomes. Most serving matelots have now never known anything but integration. Gender is a non-issue.

I had the opportunity to serve at sea in the first tranche of female sea-goers in the Royal Navy. Whilst excited at the prospect, I was slightly nervous about the reception we would face. I was pleasantly impressed with our integration on board. The Commanding Officer had shown strong leadership in briefing his ship's company to fully integrate the female personnel and to treat them as they would any other newly joined sailors. Overwhelmingly, the ship's company gave us the chance to prove our professionalism, aided by the ship's programme of operational sea training. The female personnel dug out, perhaps with a point to prove, and, despite a steep learning curve, did a good job to maintain the professional effectiveness of the ship, ensuring she was assessed as ready to deploy to a war zone in a few weeks.

Lt Gareth Harding RN (surface fleet) HMS ILLUSTRIOUS

As a superior when you're giving instruction and giving guidance, if you take time to explain, to make sure people understand what you're trying to achieve (not just the direction you're giving) then it helps them to develop their personalities and their leadership styles. If you have the ability to understand how someone's receiving your instructions then you have a better opportunity of drawing the necessary qualities from that person.

The further you come up the rank structure, the more you rely on the person next to you. Irrespective of rank structure, to a degree you always rely on the person next to you anyway, and in any situation – the situation can change immediately – you could be relying on the person next to you for a completely different reason. And as such you listen to people; you develop your skills with other people.

Cdr Steven Rogers RN (surface fleet) COMDEVFLOT

You have to have the empathy that's needed to understand the role of people at sea. There's a lot of that goes on but you hardly even notice that you're doing it. You find a ship struggling, and you're able to have a word with somebody that might just get them a little bit of support. Leadership does come into it of course, but it doesn't always look like it.

Understanding your people, understanding life at sea, understanding the privations of life at sea and the technical difficulties that life at sea imposes, say, on weapons maintenance, all these require somebody who is credible and highly experienced. We have to allow the latitude for there to be shades of grey. It's very definitely not a black and white business.

As long as you know what you're talking about, and you're confident about it, then they have no reason to doubt what you say. And if they don't understand they will ask questions. If you can answer them, that's the test.

7. Innovation

Capt Tom Buchanan RN (surface fleet) COMDEVFLOT

I'd say kick the past away at every level. Recognise that we spend an enormous amount of time growing our talent and using the indigenous strength of the people we get. I want to utilise the skills and experience and capitalise on the character of each and every man and woman. All we've got is our ability to lead, our ability to inspire in some way or other.

Surg Cdr Will Morris RN (surface fleet) PMO, HMS ILLUSTRIOUS

As a Surgeon I have two main responsibilities. The first is to look after people's health – fix them whenever they get broken, help them to get better, and to a certain extent try to stop them getting hurt. The second is to support the command aim and operational capability. For us to be successful as a Department we need to be out in other Departments. We need to be visible, engaging, available, and that's the key part of it for me. I think that our Servicemen are special and I want to do as much as I can for them. Being available is important.

The military model of leadership is standing up in front of people and saying, 'This is my plan. This is what we're going to do. This is what you're going to do for me to achieve my aim. Let's go.' That would be a fairly standard military model. You can be as dictatorial as you like but you can also do it more subtly. My style and my character are more about getting people to do things because they buy into what I want.

Col Matt Porter RM (Royal Marines) Command Wing, CTCRM Lympstone

A young Commander will find himself in interactions with inter-national NGOs, with other government agencies, with FCO reps, with other nationalities' armed forces, other agencies etc. While I was working with Afghan or Iraqi forces, or with other cultures, and not just military, I met government officials and local elders, people who hadn't necessarily got any allegiance to them or to the government. That requires a different sort of leadership. It's still leadership, you're still trying to exert an influence over those people but the process isn't eased by the fact that you're in a position of authority.

This is the matter of authority versus leadership. The natural definition of command is all about authority; you're in the rank and therefore you have the authority and therefore things happen. Well, that's great. But that's command. This isn't command; this is an interaction between you and somebody else. So in terms of leadership there is need for a great diversity of leadership styles.

Lt Gareth Tennant RM (Royal Marines) FPGRM, Faslane

My perception of leadership is purely from commanding Marines on the ground. Dealing with a difficult situation is easy. The preparation to get you there is hard. Once you get to that difficult situation where those decisions need to be made the training takes over. You do it the way you've been taught and the way you've practised; as long as you've got the professional knowledge behind you, that is the easy bit.

As situations change on the ground, the reaction of the Navy is going to have to be faster, and the decisions that are going to need to be made are going to be a lot more instinctive, and therefore at a much lower level. At higher level it's always going to be the same – planning and preparation. But the training has to be in place so that at lower level people can make decisions faster and have the confidence that they are in a position to make those decisions. That means Mission Command is completely essential.

As we move into more asymmetric warfare, we'll find that Mission Command becomes more and more prevalent. Actually we need to rely on people of all ranks to be able to make decisions and therefore they need to realise beforehand that they may find themselves in these positions. But also the chain of command needs to empower people to make these decisions so they can feel confident that they are doing the right thing.

8. Integrity

Lt Lee Beeching RN (surface fleet) HMS ILLUSTRIOUS

A good leader leads by example. That is, by leadership in his bearing, his dignity. His integrity is vital. So if you want to be a good leader, people have got to respect you; the big thing is integrity. If you want them to be correct in their behaviour, then your behaviour must be of an even higher standard.

Admiral the Lord Boyce (Mike) (submariner) Chief of Defence Staff

Qualities like integrity and not stabbing people in the back (not our culture in the Armed Forces, on the whole) or trying to climb over other people to get to where you're trying to go, are strengths clearly recognised.

Integrity is very important, as is a high degree of endurance and stamina such that you aren't getting flaky when you get tired. And having the confidence to ask people what they think is important. I rate, as equally important, good manners, singularly lacking in society now. As a leader you should be well mannered and not sharp, show appreciation of something which is done; these attributes are lacking among some of our senior public hierarchy today. But not in the Armed Forces, that comes under cheerfulness and respect for others; and we do that well.

Lt Anna Harvey RN (fleet air arm) 829 NAS

I treat everyone as I would like to be treated. My team will actually come to see me when they've done something wrong because they know I'll be disappointed in what they've done. I'm consistent; they know where they stand with me and they don't see any kind of confusion within my style. The key thing is consistency – or integrity. That's been true all the way through my career. You need to know that it is down to you.

PO Dave Rouse (surface fleet) HMS IRON DUKE

We want our people to develop their own leadership styles. You can't have thirty clones of the instructor. Everybody has their own way of getting things done, but the ownership still has to be with them to get that job done. It is strength of character we're looking for.

'Strength of character' is a term for a range of moral values that are more in evidence here than in other environments. People seem to be more honest, more respectful, on better behaviour, of better character. Personal integrity is at the heart of what we do.

9. Moral and physical courage

Admiral Sir Jonathon Band (surface fleet) First Sea Lord and Chief of the Naval Staff (2007–09)

The leadership challenge for us is that while we reflect society and while we abide by the norms of society, we're still asked to do extraordinary things. Our ethos and our values perpetuate the style of Royal Navy that we have.

The more extreme areas of activity like the Royal Marines, the front end of flying, the deep end of diving, and the submarine operations are collectively extremely brave and courageous. They're trained. And they're given additional training to make them like that. They understand the environment they're in, there's a very big strength of safety culture in the Submarine Service, because if anything goes wrong, the submarine goes down. There is a strong safety culture in the Fleet Air Arm. They are all trained together, and so their threshold of leadership challenge may be different – I wouldn't mark it up or down – than more general activity, which may be less stressful on a day-to-day basis. That might be on a surface ship or onshore; but when it gets extreme, it gets extreme very quickly.

There are at the moment 500 sailors doing 'general military duties' on land: everything from logistics, to medical, to driving trucks, to repairing trucks, to doing top cover on convoys going out down the roads in Afghanistan.

Capt Stephen Hart RM (Royal Marines) Command Wing, CTCRM Lympstone

Moral courage. This comes when there are difficult decisions to be made. There is normally an easy answer or an answer that isn't the right thing but which would get you out of the immediate problem; it's morally courageous to say: 'We're not going to do that. We're going to do the right thing,' and for people to say, 'OK,' and in essence, agree with you and follow you.

Lt Cdr David Jones RN (submarine fleet) MEO, HMS TRENCHANT

The moral element describes the intangible. In other situations you might call it 'faith;' it attempts to explain why somebody does something that makes no logical sense, why they suddenly put themselves back into a fire to pull someone out, at considerable personal risk to themselves, and possibly to the ship. Why does somebody stay in a flooded engine room physically damaging themselves? There's the moral component of leadership: having moral courage, having the integrity to do what you think is right based on your judgement is important, but that doesn't mean we sit around talking about rights and wrongs: it just happens.

PO Jules Lee (surface fleet) RNLA

I would define the moral component as a kind of camaraderie. Being in the Navy to me is like being part of something. There's nothing better for me than being able to say, 'I'm in the Navy.' I'm not looking forward to leaving. I will be gutted saying, 'I'm an electrician.' I like to say 'I'm in the Navy.' It doesn't matter what you are in the Navy, just the fact of saying to somebody 'I'm in the Navy,' is what makes me proud.

10. Professional knowledge

Admiral the Lord Boyce (Mike) (submariner) Chief of
Defence Staff

Any leader should understand what he or she is actually driving,
whether a ship or a battalion, a machine or a human organisation.
Knowing what you're talking about inculcates confidence in the
people you are leading and gives you the confidence to know that
what you're asking people to do is a possibility.

Cdr Kieran O'Brien RN (fleet air arm) Commander Air
Engineer, HMS ILLUSTRIOUS

Aviation is a peculiar discipline. There are absolutes, there's no
doubt; airworthiness and flight safety are absolutes. But there's an
element of risk management that comes into leadership and how
you deliver your output. You have to know where those absolutes are
set. If you kept working for perfection you'd burn people out. You've
got to know where that line is between absolute safety and 'risk-
managed safety'. We would never be unsafe. The people I work with
and the people I lead are very cognisant of the rules. And I reinforce
that. Standards and practices are my responsibility in this ship, and I
will always tell people: 'You must adhere to the absolute.'

But what I also look for is a discussion and a leadership responsibility.

It's all about risk management and knowing the rules inside out. You always have to consider the context. 'What are we here for?' We are here to take risk. We are here to deliver that effect. We work on military effect and we need to be out there doing our business otherwise we are not doing anything at all. And you have to know your professional responsibility. I value professionalism, judgement, and fortitude – morally and physically – to be able to follow that through and make those hard calls. And that is what people would see as leadership.

Capt Kempley Smith Rifles CTCRM Lympstone

The Combat Estimate and the Tactical Aide Memoir are useful and powerful leadership tools. But as with all things, especially in the military, it's easy to become institutionalised or blinkered so that you just follow the process. If you're constrained by them you prevent yourself from thinking outside the box. So you need to be able to use these things, understand how they work. If they don't fit the plan that you're using you need to be able to alter it absolutely so that whatever you're looking to achieve can be done, even if it doesn't fit what you've been taught is the best way. That's why it's called an 'aide memoir' rather a 'must'. You don't have to follow it slavishly;

it's just an aid to help you think about all these various factors. Some are good aids yet sometimes they don't always fit every problem that you've got and you need to be intellectually sensible enough to be flexible.

It is the development of military analysis, being able to problem solve, and then to clearly and concisely direct it, and pass on the information to your subordinates. Your role is to be the intellectual leader, and your people should look up to you because of your intellect, because when it comes down to it and everything goes wrong it's up to you the leader to come up with a plan. That's the key thing.

11. Stamina

Lt Ken Bailes RN (surface fleet) HMS ILLUSTRIOUS

It is easier in the Ops Room when it's busy. The Ops Room environment is laid out. It's evident who is in charge; but if it's not, something has broken down. There's more flexibility in how it manifests itself, but leading by example is the way forward. The key is in knowing where you need to push people and where you need to keep their interest. I give both direction and guidance. It's harder, really, when it's quiet. In training we make it as realistic as possible but it's not the real thing. And yet when you put people in the real thing they're 100% focused on what they're doing.

Lt Ben Chappell RM (Royal Marines) CTCRM Lympstone

We have to be robust as leaders. You have to be the guy who is reliable, who's able to carry a heavy Bergen, or who's always going to have some idea of the tactics of the situation. It's not just the physical stamina that is important, it's the mental and also the tactical awareness as well, and ultimately political.

You've got to be determined. But when it really does get hard cheerfulness is definitely a big quality: if you let things get to you then you're going to affect the blokes around you as well.

Lt Nicholas Joseph RM (Royal Marines) CTCRM Lympstone

Strong beliefs underpin everything: having a strong frame of mind. It's not about eloquence; it's not about how many qualifications you have, or if you have a Bachelors or a Masters degree; it's not even about how you carry yourself. It is about being steadfast. You have to believe in yourself and have a strong frame of mind simply to carry on whatever task you're given. Once your people see that you have a strong mind as a leader and that you continue, you persevere no matter what, they will look up to you and respect you.

Cdr Peter Olive RN (surface fleet) Commanding Officer, HMS ARGYLL

Being the decisive person is a role that's grown on me over the years, more and more as I've settled into the environment and grown more confident. The challenges are multifarious. That's what makes it a good day at the office. And that, in part, is what leadership in command is about. If you wake up in the morning and think: 'So many things to overcome!' then you're not in the right job. Whereas if you think, 'So many things to overcome, looks like an exciting challenge' then this is the job for you.

Ships' captains must have an understanding of dynamics of scale; something you get with wisdom and age. There's a fascinating quote, 'Nothing more dangerous to Her Majesty's policy than one of Her Majesty's ship's captains afloat at sea.' If you get it wrong one ship can really embarrass the government very quickly. It is vital to understand why that is the case and to grasp the dynamics of the political/military space.

Lt Cdr Jim Parrott RN (surface fleet) Lt Cdr RN, XO HMS EDINBURGH

Action comes infrequently; but the training has to be there, and the observation has to be there, and the attention has to be there too. These are matters of stamina. It might be a maritime threat or threat to the guys on the ground in Afghanistan and Iraq. One of the attributes of the air threat is the speed and the brevity of the action. For the time you spend potentially in a war situation, 99.9% of the time nothing will be happening. It's that 0.1% where it is happening. That's the bit that you've got to pick up. Everyone needs to be sharp enough to deal with it and not miss it.

12. Trust

WO1 Gary Nicolson (submarine fleet) HMS ILLUSTRIOUS

Submariners understand their function on board. Because of the fact that we live in such tight confines, we all know the rank structure; if someone tells you to do something you do it. We trust each other implicitly. Very rarely do you ask any questions unless you deem it unsafe or you're unsure of what you've got to do; in which case: 'Can you just explain that? Can you tell me what you require from me?' And we have that culture anyway inbuilt. There's no such thing as a stupid question in submarines. That's a general rule.

The best way of describing it is that we are reactors. If the Captain or the Officer of the Watch gives an order, especially in the Control Room, it's reactive and it happens. But it's also in the

manner in which it's delivered. In certain scenarios you could cut
the atmosphere with a knife. And in others the atmosphere is quite
relaxing. It depends on the situation.

Cpl Thomas O'Sullivan (Royal Marines) FPGRM

Working in small teams you can trust people. You do not have to
run around after people. You could be trusting your life to others,
especially boarding vessels. Most of our boardings are compliant
and even if they're non-compliant are a low threat; but there is a
threat, especially in that environment, and you've got to be able to
trust the lad shooting right next to you engaging targets. If it does
go wrong you can trust that he can make the right decision, the right
call in that millisecond to drop that target. And they've got to have a
trust in me to make the right tactical decision. So trust has got to be
both ways – they've got to trust you to make the right decision, and
I've got to trust them to be able to carry out my decision. The way I
approach leadership is to give all my men the responsibilities. Give
them as much responsibility as you can possibly give and they will
meet those responsibilities.

It's the same with me looking to officers. I've got to be able to
trust on a more conventional scheme, on a Section attack, or Troop
attack, that the Troop Officer has made the right decision in how

we're going to assault the position. As long as you've got trust there you know he's not going to make the wrong call. He's going to make the right call, and it's going to save lives.

Cdre Jon Westbrook RN (surface fleet) The Commodore, DEVFLOT

The same principles of leadership apply at the flotilla level as they do at the unit level: understanding the individuals (because everyone commands in a different way), and understanding which techniques can be brought to bear to enhance their performance. Whatever level of leadership you're exercising, or whatever level you're exercising leadership, taking time and trouble to understand people as individuals to whom you are delivering the direction/leadership, advice or guidance is time very well spent.

One of the most difficult things in command – at sea, in particular – is knowing how much you can trust people whom you know nothing about. You can join a ship and take command in a foreign port the day the ship sails. You will have discussed individuals with your predecessor, but you will not have seen the way in which your officers perform.

GLOSSARY OF TERMS

AB	Able Rating
Brig	Brigadier
BRNC	Britannia Royal Naval College
Capt	Captain
Cdr	Commander
Cdre	Commodore
Col	Colonel
Cpl	Corporal
CO	Commanding Officer
COMDEVFLOT	Commodore Devonport Flotilla
CPO	Chief Petty Officer
CTC RM	Commando Training Centre Royal Marines
LH	Leading Hand
Lt	Lieutenant
Lt Cdr	Lieutenant Commander
Lt Col	Lieutenant Colonel
Maj	Major
MTCD	Maritime Through Career Development
PO	Petty Officer
PT	Physical Trainer

PWO	Principal Warfare Officer
RM	Royal Marines
RN	Royal Navy
RNLA	Royal Naval Leadership Academy
Sgt	Sergeant
XO	Executive Officer (Second in Command)
WO1	Warrant Officer (First Class)
WO2	Warrant Officer (Second Class)

ACKNOWLEDGEMENTS

A book of this nature, scale and scope is hardly the work of only one person. Over the last three years I have interviewed – or rather listened to and overheard – hundreds of people (individually and in groups), read many thousands of pages of leadership doctrine and thinking, and accumulated millions of words of evidence. This book is a short, concentrated version of the largest survey of its kind ever commissioned by the Royal Navy.

My research is also by definition subject to the most rigorous peer review at every stage. Nothing here has evaded scrutiny of the best kind. Of course, beyond that assurance, some readers may be interested in the methodology and heuristic nature of my research, in the questions asked, in the evidence adduced, in the leadership theories accounted for, and in the broad, deep reading in the subject on which any book of this kind must depend. Other readers might expect to find the extensive footnotes, endnotes, bibliography, appendices or other apparatus that might ordinarily accompany research of this scale. I can supply those data to readers should they wish to write to me with specific requests; but here is not the place: this is not that kind of book.

*   *   *

I owe great thanks to many people:

None of this would have been possible without the financial support of Babcock International and its shareholders. Its CEO, Peter Rogers, has been immensely helpful and I have enjoyed working with him, with Derah McCall and their team.

To all those in the Royal Navy who have contributed in person or in writing I am deeply grateful. In thanking Mark Stanhope and Charles Montgomery not only for their individual support of the book, but also in their formal roles as First and Second Sea Lord, I hope to convey just how highly I value the enthusiastic and informed help that I received in every quarter of the Royal Navy. In thanking them, I thank everyone.

Everywhere I was made to feel welcome; everywhere the project was understood, refined and improved; everywhere I met individuals of outstanding professional and moral standing. I should particularly like to thank: Mark Anderson, Sarah Barton, Colin Bauld, Lee Beeching, Neil Bennett, Andy Beverley, Russ Billings, Dave Brickell, Paul Brookes, Tom Buchanan, Steve Chick, Tim Cordery, Martin Douglass, Bill Dunham, Joel Durbridge, Mike Farrage, Ian Fitter, Phil Gilby, John Gray, Tim Hall, Andy Hancock, Angie Hancock, Stephen Hart, Anna Harvey, Victoria Hobby, Laurie Hopkins, Jim Hutton, Tim Johnston, Nicholas Joseph, Mark Kerr, Jules Lee, Pete Maskell, Will Morris, Jim Mozeley, Alan Neckrews, Gary Nicolson, Billy May,

Will Northcott, Kieran O'Brien, Thomas O'Sullivan, Peter Olive, Alec Parry, Ian Perryman, Jonathan Phelps, Dale Randle, Dave Rouse, Hugo Sedgwick, James Shortall, Kempley Smith, Chris Snow, Doug Spencer, Charlotte Taylor, Gareth Tennant, Amy Tomlinson, Richard Turrell, Richard Voller, Rory West and Tim Wright. All provided the insights and the peer review from experts and practitioners that helped shape the book and its credibility.

John Adair kindly allowed permission to reprint his seminal Action Centred Leadership. Marion Haberhauer was the most patient and accurate of transcribers.

Others have been vitally helpful to the project as a whole, and have made this book possible in many ways. I owe them my deep thanks: James Burnell-Nugent for the initial idea and for constant cheerful support; Jonathon Band for understanding the scope of the project; Stephen Mackay for his resilience, persistence and foresight; Nigel Langhorn and Gareth Hughes for making everything possible within the Royal Navy, and Nick Harland at Flagship; Lawson Tickell for help at Culdrose and Colin Nicklas and Karl Santrian at RNLA; Richard Ibbotson and Tim McClement for reading early drafts, and Alan Massey and Jake Moores for advice on the content of later ones; Chris Snow and Clive Johnstone for help at FOST; Andy Lock and Matt Porter for making me welcome at Lympstone over many months and for their invaluable intellectual and ethical contributions; Ged Salzano for reading and editing later drafts; Ed Chacksfield for his capable and intellectually generous help; Jeff Wright for proofreading; Geoff Wintle for handling the finances; Russ Haines for his vital editorial contributions, and finally Simon Williams who steered this project through its final stages and who judged the tone and scope of the book exactly and expertly – I owe him a particular debt of thanks.

The publishers, designers, printers and marketers at Random House, under the cheerful leadership of Trevor Dolby and Nicola Taplin, were a pleasure to work with. Jonathan Lloyd of Curtis Brown was a constant source of wisdom and wit on this as on many other books I have written. My wife, Mary Loudon, and our daughters, Clare, Jane and Celia have been patient during my many absences on Navy business, and loving on my returns: one of the many patterns of naval life.

INDEX

(numbers in italic indicate tables and diagrams)

Action Centred Leadership (ACL) 75, *76*, 139
Adair, John 76, 139
air power, wide diversity in the use of 48
Air Squadrons, *see* Naval Air Squadrons (NAS)
Air Warfare 43
Amundsen, Roald 1
Anderson, Rear Admiral Mark 101–2, 138
Argyll, HMS 22, 76, 110, 131
Ashby, Lt Maxine Kim 80
assessment of risk 36, 60
Aviation 38, 43, 127

Bailes, Lt Ken 129
Band, Admiral Sir Jonathon 124–5, 139
Beeching, Lt Lee 122, 138
behaviours 5, 7, 12, 25, 40, 45, 55, 64, 65, 66, 78
   range of 65–7
Bennett, WO1 Neil 111, 138
Billings, WO1 Russ 108–9, 138
Boyce, Admiral the Lord (Mike) 122–3, 127
Briant-Evans, Lt Cdr Zoe 32

Britannia Royal Naval College (BRNC), *see* Dartmouth, BRNC
BRNC Dartmouth, *see* Dartmouth, BRNC
Buchanan, Capt Tom 119, 138
Burnell-Nugent, Admiral Sir James 2, 107, 139
Burnell, Lt Col Jeremy 99
Burr, Capt Chris 46
Burrell, Lt Cdr Dave 51

'can-do' attitude 23–4
capacity for judgement and decision making, as a leadership quality 56
   insights on 101–5
Chadfield, Lt Cdr Laurence 27
Chappell, Lt Ben 130
cheerfulness, as a leadership quality 56
   insights on 105–6
clarity and vision, as a leadership quality 57
   insights on 107–8
Clewes, Lt Sarah 76
climate change 87, 88, 90
coaching 81–5
   boundaries of 83–4
   four elements of 83

GROW model of 84, *84*
  mentoring contrasted to 85
  techniques for 84, *84*
  'tell' style vs 'ask' approach of 83
Collingwood, HMS 2, 31, 100
Combat Estimate 88, 128
command, naval definition of 64, 65
Commando Training Centre Royal
  Marines (CTCRM), *see* Lympstone,
  CTCRM 82
communication skills, as a leadership
  quality 57
  insights on 108–10
competencies *65*, *66*
confidence, as a leadership quality 58
  fostering 39, 58
  insights on 111–14
Connerton, LOM(C) Natasha 115
Cordery, PO Tim 31, 138
CTCRM Lympstone, *see* Lympstone,
  CTCRM
C2DRIL, *see* Six Core Values
  (C2DRIL)
Culdrose, RNAS 2, 49, 139

Dartmouth, BRNC 2, 12, 27, 41, 51, 76,
  97
Defence Academy, Shrivenham 2
Devonport Flotilla (DEVFLOT) 118,
  119, 134
Divisional System 69–70
  as 'family in the workplace' 69
  robust nature of 70

'Dolphins' 50
Dunham, Brig Bill 44–5, 138

Edinburgh, HMS 131
829 NAS 123
emotional intelligence 1, 4
Estimate Process 49–50
European Union (EU) 89
Everest, Mount 1

Finn, Lt Cdr Stuart 'Sharky' 107–8
Fleet Air Arm 48–50
  leadership within 48
  multi-role combat capability 48
Force Protection Group Royal Marines
  (FPGRM) 99, 121, 133
Foreign and Commonwealth Office
  (FCO) 120
FPGRM, Faslane, *see* Force Protection
  Group Royal Marines (FPGRM)
Functional Leadership, *see* Action
  Centred Leadership (ACL)
future leadership 87–93
  trends influencing 87, 89–90

Garrow, LOM Peter 35
global inequality 87
global media, *see* media
globalisation 87
Gray, Lt Cdr John 102–3, 111–12, 138
Greenly-Jones, CPO Paul 13
GROW model 84, *84*

Haines, Lt Cdr Russ 100–1
Hall, PO Tim 47, 138
Hancock, Cdr Andy 41
Harding, Lt Gareth 117–18
Hart, Capt Stephen 115–16, 125, 138
Harvey, Lt Anna 123, 138
Hillary, Sir Edmund 1
Hobby, Victoria 112, 138
humanity and humility, as a leadership
    quality 58
        insights on 115–19
humour 21–2
Hurworth, HMS 23, 36, 47
Hutton, Col Jim 82, 87, 138

Illustrious, HMS 38, 39, 68, 98, 104, 108,
    112, 115, 117, 119, 122, 127, 129, 132
innovation, as a leadership quality 59
        insights on 119–22
insights, *see* leadership, insights
integrity, as a leadership quality 59
        insights on 122–4
        and knowing 99
international security, trends in 87,
    89–90
Iron Duke, HMS 124

Jones, Lt Cdr David 112–13, 126
Joseph, Lt Nicholas 130, 138

Kelley, Lt Alexandra 49
knowing
    and integrity 99

others 1, 4
in risk management 128
and stamina 129
and teamwork 61
who to trust 134
yourself 1

Lacey, Lt Cdr Cathy 116–17
leaderless tasks 79
leadership:
    behaviours 5, 7, 12, 25, 40, 45, 55,
        64–7, 65, 66, 78
    cheerfulness 3–4, 56, 105–6
    clarity and vision 3, 57, 107–8
    common-sense approach to 78
    communication skills 57, 108–10
    confidence 21, 39, 41, 42, 49, 56, 58,
        111–14
    essential skills and qualities for 79
    ethical or moral content of 3
    ethos 6
    future of 87–93
        competence in 92–3
    grounded principles of 3
    insights 6, 95–134
        Anderson, Rear Admiral Mark
            101–2
        Ashby, Lt Maxine Kim 80
        Bailes, Lt Ken 129
        Band, Admiral Sir Jonathon
            124–5
        Beeching, Lt Lee 122
        Bennett, WO1 Neil 111

leadership, insights (*continued*):
    Billings, WO1 Russ 108–9
    Boyce, Admiral the Lord (Mike)
        122–3, 127
    Briant-Evans, Lt Cdr Zoe 32
    Buchanan, Capt Tom 119
    Burnell-Nugent, Admiral Sir
        James 107
    Burnell, Lt Col Jeremy 99
    Burr, Capt Chris 46
    Burrell, Lt Cdr Dave 51
    Chadfield, Lt Cdr Laurence 27
    Chappell, Lt Ben 130
    Clewes, Lt Sarah 76
    Connerton, LOM(C) Natasha
        115
    Cordery, PO Tim 31
    Dunham, Brig Bill 44–5
    Finn, Lt Cdr Stuart 'Sharky'
        107–8
    Garrow, LOM Peter 35
    Gray, Lt Cdr John 102–3, 111–12
    Greenly-Jones, CPO Paul 13
    Haines, Lt Cdr Russ 100–1
    Hall, PO Tim 47
    Hancock, Cdr Andy 41
    Harding, Lt Gareth 117–18
    Hart, Capt Stephen 125
    Hart Capt Stephen 115–16
    Harvey, Lt Anna 123
    Hobby, Victoria 112
    Hutton, Col Jim 82, 87
    Jones, Lt Cdr David 112–13, 126

leadership, insights (*continued*):
    Joseph, Lt Nicholas 130
    Kelley, Lt Alexandra 49
    Lacey, Lt Cdr Cathy 116–17
    Lee, PO Jules 126
    Lock, Maj Andy 96–7
    Mackay, Cdr Stephen 103–4
    May, CPO Billy 68
    Milne, PO Bruce 98
    Morris, Surg Cdr Will 119–20
    Morton, PO Ady 22
    Nekrews, Lt Alan 23–4
    Nicklas, Lt Cdr Colin 109–10
    Nicolson, WO1 Gary 132–3
    Northcott, Capt Will 105–6
    O'Brien, Cdr Kieran 38, 127–8
    Olive, Cdr Peter 131
    O'Sullivan, Cpl Thomas 133–4
    Parrott, Lt Cdr Jim 131–2
    Parry, Cdr Alec 39–40
    Porter, Col Matt 120–1
    Rogers, Cdr Steven 118–19
    Rouse, PO Dave 124
    Sedgwick, Lt Hugo 99–100
    Short, Cdr Jeff 12
    Shortall, Lt James 104–5
    Smith, Capt Kempley 128–9
    Stanhope, Admiral Sir Mark 54
    Starbuck, WO2 Tony 36
    Storton, Lt George 106
    Tennant, Lt Gareth 121–2
    Titterton, Capt Philip 113–14
    Voller, PO Richard 114

leadership, insights (*continued*):
    Walmsley, Cdr Liz 20–1
    West, Lt Cdr Rory 110
    Westbrook, Cdre Jon 134
    Williams, Cmdre Simon 10–11
    Wright, Lt Cdr Tim 97–8
  naval definition of 64, 65
  qualities, twelve types of, *see* Twelve
    Leadership Qualities
  'soft skills' 1, 4
  at strategic level 88
    fundamental questions of 89
  styles, 67
    types of 48–50, 75–85
  thinking 75–80, 76
    seven-point checklist 77–8
  tools for 29–32
  views on, *see* insights
Leadership Tools 29–32
Leading Hand 34, 35
Lee, PO Jules 126, 138
Lock, Maj Andy 96–7
Lympstone, CTCRM 2, 44, 82, 87, 96,
  105, 115, 120, 125, 128, 130, 139

Mackay, Cdr Stephen 103–4, 139
management, naval definition of 64,
  65
Maritime Estimate 6, 88
Maritime Tactical Estimate (MTE) 29
  and Mission Command 30
  phases of:
    Analysis 29

commander's decision 29
Course of Action development
  and validation 29
Seven Questions of 29, 79
Maritime Through Career Development
  (MTCD) framework 5, 71–5, 71–5, 82
May, CPO Billy 68, 138
media 89, 91, 92
mentoring, coaching contrasted to 85
Milne, PO Bruce 98
Ministry of Defence (MOD) 113
Mission Command 29–30, 32
  essence of 2–3
moral and physical courage, as a
  leadership quality 60
    fostering 60
    insights on 124–6
Morris, Surg Cdr Will 119–20, 138
Morton, PO Ady 22
MTCD, *see* Maritime Through Career
  Development (MTCD) framework
MTE, *see* Maritime Tactical Estimate
  (MTE)

NATO 89
NATO Sequence of Orders (NSOs)
  30–2, 79
Naval Air Squadrons (NAS) 11, 107, 123
  structure of 49
Naval Home Command 107
naval personnel views on leadership, *see*
  leadership, insights
naval terms, glossary of 135–6

Nekrews, Lt Alan 23–4, 138
Nelson, Vice-Admiral Horatio Lord 2
Nelson's Trafalgar Memorandum 2
NGOs 89, 92, 120
NSOs, see NATO Sequence of Orders
    (NSOs)
Nicklas, Lt Cdr Colin 109–10, 139
Nicolson, WO1 Gary 132–3, 138
Northcott, Capt Will 103–4, 105–6, 139
O'Brien, Cdr Kieran 38, 127–8, 139
Ocean, HMS 80
Olive, Cdr Peter 131, 139
O'Sullivan, Cpl Thomas 133–4, 139

Parrott, Lt Cdr Jim 131–2
Parry, Cdr Alec 39–40, 139
Perisher Course 104
personnel views on leadership, see
    leadership, insights
Porter, Col Matt 120–1, 139
Practical Leadership Tasks (PLTs) 104
Principal Warfare Officer (PWO) 43
professional knowledge, as a leadership
    quality 60–1
    insights on 127–9
Protector, HMS 35
psychological insight 1
Puncher, HMS 106

Raleigh, HMS 2, 13
respect for others 1, 4
risk assessment 36, 60
risk management 127, 128

RNAS Culdrose, see Culdrose, RNAS
RNLA, see Royal Navy Leadership
    Academy (RNLA)
Rogers, Cdr Steven 118–19
Rouse, PO Dave 124, 139
Royal Marines 44–8
    ethos of 6, 45–6
Royal Navy Diversity and Inclusion 20
Royal Navy Leadership Academy
    (RNLA) 32, 46, 75, 100, 109, 111, 114,
    126, 139

Scott, Robert 1
Sedgwick, Lt Hugo 99–100, 139
Senior Ratings Command Course
    (SRCC) 114
771 NAS 107
Shackleton, Ernest 1, 4
ship 11
    as community of people 33–4
    teams within 43
        'tribal' characteristics of 43
Short, Cdr Jeff 12
Shortall, Lt James 104–5, 139
Situational Leadership 75
Six Core Values (C2DRIL) 5, 9–24,
    42, 82
    aspects of 21–4
        'can-do' attitude 23–4
        humour 21–2
        teamwork 22
    commitment 3, 14–15, 96–7
    courage 3, 15, 97–8

determination 20
discipline 3, 16, 98
expressed in individuals 95–6
insights on 96–101
integrity 3, 18, 99–100
loyalty 3, 19–20, 100–1
moral, ethical and spiritual
    dimensions of 12
respect for others 3, 17, 99
Royal Marine ethos equates to 45–6
on submarines 52
Smith, Capt Kempley 128–9, 139
'soft skills' 4
    emphasis on 1
stamina, as a leadership quality 61–2
    insights on 129–32
    and knowing 129
Stanhope, Admiral Sir Mark 54, 138
Starbuck, WO2 Tony 36
Storton, Lt George 106
Submarine Command Course 111
submarines 2, 11, 50–2
    as community of people 33, 51–2
    'Dolphins' earned onboard 50
    ethos on 52
    priority of safety on 50
    Six Core Values (C2DRIL) on 52
    style of leadership on 50–2
Surface Flotilla 43–4
Surface Warfare 43

Tactical Estimate, see Maritime Tactical
    Estimate (MTE)

teamwork 22
    and knowing 61
Tennant, Lt Gareth 121, 121–2, 139
thinking, leadership 75–80, 76
    seven-point checklist for 77–8
Titterton, Capt Philip 113–14
Trenchant, HMS 99, 111, 112, 126
trust, as a leadership quality 62
    fostering 34
    insights on 132–4
    knowing who to 134
Twelve Leadership Qualities 5, 53–62,
    82
    capacity for judgement and decision
        making 56, 101–5
    cheerfulness 56, 105–6
    clarity and vision 57, 107–8
    communication skills 57, 108–10
    confidence 58, 111–14
    expressed in individuals 95–6
    humanity and humility 58, 115–19
    innovation 59, 119–22
    insights on 101–34
    integrity 59, 122–4
    moral and physical courage 60,
        124–6
    professional knowledge 60–1,
        127–9
    stamina 61–2, 129–32
    trust 62, 132–4

UK High Level Operational Concept
    91–2

Underwater Warfare 43
United Nations (UN) 89

Vengeance, HMS 102
views on leadership, *see* leadership, insights
Voller, PO Richard 114, 139

Walmsley, Cdr Liz 20–1
warfare disciplines, types of 43
warfare effort, teams support 43
West, Lt Cdr Rory 110, 139
Westbrook, Cdre Jon 134
Williams, Cmdre Simon 10–11, 140
Wright, Lt Cdr Tim 97–8, 139